CAMBRIDGE IBERIAN AND
LATIN AMERICAN STUDIES

GENERAL EDITOR

PROFESSOR P. E. RUSSELL, F.B.A.

PROFESSOR OF SPANISH STUDIES, THE UNIVERSITY OF OXFORD

The Krausist Movement
and ideological change in Spain,
1854–1874

The Krausist Movement
and ideological change in Spain,
1854–1874

JUAN LÓPEZ-MORILLAS

ASHBEL SMITH PROFESSOR OF SPANISH
UNIVERSITY OF TEXAS AT AUSTIN

TRANSLATED BY FRANCES M. LÓPEZ-MORILLAS

CAMBRIDGE UNIVERSITY PRESS

CAMBRIDGE

LONDON   NEW YORK   NEW ROCHELLE

MELBOURNE   SYDNEY

CAMBRIDGE UNIVERSITY PRESS
Cambridge, New York, Melbourne, Madrid, Cape Town, Singapore,
São Paulo, Delhi, Dubai, Tokyo

Cambridge University Press
The Edinburgh Building, Cambridge CB2 8RU, UK

Published in the United States of America by Cambridge University Press, New York

www.cambridge.org
Information on this title: www.cambridge.org/9780521135313

A catalogue record for this publication is available from the British Library

ISBN 978-0-521-23256-2 Hardback
ISBN 978-0-521-13531-3 Paperback

Contents

General Editor's Foreword

Professor López-Morillas's classic study, first published in Spanish in 1956 under the title *El Krausismo español*, involves a comprehensive examination of what has been described as 'the bizarre phenomenon' of Krausism in nineteenth-century Spain. Bizarre as its ideology and the circumstances of its arrival in Spain may have been, 'Krausism' had a great deal to do with forming the outlook and preoccupations of the radical element in Spanish life at that time. It originated in the middle of the century when some university-connected Spanish intellectuals, reformist by inclination and totally at odds with the, as they thought, irrational, decadent and self-seeking forces that then ruled Spanish politics and society, nevertheless felt themselves without access to any acceptable system of ideas capable of giving coherence and purpose to their radical urges. They found what they were looking for when a professor of philosophy at the University of Madrid, Julián Sanz del Río, returned to Spain in the 1840s as a fervent disciple of the philosophy of a now quite forgotten minor post-Kantian German idealist thinker, Karl Christian Friedrich Krause (1781–1830). Though even Sanz del Río himself was never able to explain effectively to his Spanish lecture audiences the full meaning of the metaphysical complexities and the arid terminology of Krause's thought, the latter's stress on the central role of ethics in all aspects of human conduct and its preoccupation with lofty-sounding concepts such as, for example, 'harmonic rationalism', inspired a whole generation of radical intellectuals. The heyday of Krausism was in the period 1850–1880, but it had a major and enduring influence on Spanish political and social thinking, on educational theory and practice and on attitudes to religion. The impact of Krausist thinking on individual behaviour is also clearly to be seen in the work of the two greatest Spanish nineteenth-century novelists, Pérez Galdós and Leopoldo Alas. The movement was deeply repugnant to and often violently attacked by the

vii

various traditionalist forces in the state and notably by the Church, which saw the Krausists as a kind of dangerously unorthodox lay priesthood whose beliefs and moral fervour were, as was indeed the case, based on premises alien to Spanish traditions. Nevertheless, the 'New Philosophy' (as some of its adherents called it) heralded a continuing admiration for German philosophy and German science which would, even when Krausism itself had lost its appeal as an ideology, remain an important influence on the history of ideas in Spain into the twentieth century.

Professor López-Morillas's study of the subject is notable for the way in which it combines comprehensiveness with clarity and readability. Though the author's main concern is with the pervasive influence of Krausism on various aspects of the Spanish scene and with the kind of life-style it imposed on its adherents as individuals, he also successfully undertakes the difficult task of explaining the most important characteristics of Krause's philosophy. The book's appearance in an English translation will, it is hoped, make it easier for English-speaking students of nineteenth-century Europe to understand what is often seen by foreigners as a baffling element in the making of modern Spain. Professor López-Morillas, after many years as professor of Spanish and then as professor of Comparative Literature at Brown University, is now the holder of a chair in the University of Texas at Austin.

April 1980   P. E. RUSSELL

Preface to the English edition

In the following pages I have tried to present a movement of ideas that has rightly been considered one of the most influential in the history of modern Spanish thought. The reader who knows little of that history may be surprised to learn that a movement originating as the arbitrary choice of one man would later develop into a philosophical school, closely connected at first with the University of Madrid, and would eventually become a way of understanding and interpreting life that affected many Spaniards who knew little or nothing about philosophy. Today, when we have at our disposal a broad range of bibliographical data concerning the Krausist movement, we know that its remarkable influence was due neither to the novelty of its postulates nor to its intrinsic power of persuasion, but rather to the fact that it arrived in Spain from an obscure German source just at the time when an incipient intellectual class was feverishly seeking a faith or doctrine with which to identify. I believe that this is extremely important. It is well known, of course, that there were *intellectuals* – the so-called 'enlightened' men – in Spain during the eighteenth century; men, that is, who confronted the environment in which they lived and used their intelligence (they would have preferred to call it reason) to deal with that environment. But these men, first of all, worked in scattered fashion; their only point of contact was a vague feeling of reverence for *les lumières*; and in addition, they never made clear whether they thought of reason as a passive faculty, in the manner of a magnifying glass to see things better, even perhaps to observe what did not conform to 'rational order', or whether it was an active faculty, namely a structure of principles or ideas which, changed into a plan of action, would eventually supplant the traditional order of things.

Perhaps if the anti-Gallic feeling produced by the French Revolution, first, and later by the Napoleonic invasion, had been less virulent, these early intimations of critical rationalism might also have been those of an *intellectual class* that recognized itself as such and felt a responsibility for undertaking reforms. But this 'possible Spain', as the country during the reign of Charles III (1759–1788) has been described, remained just that, a mere possibility. Most of Spain's population was suspicious of the ideas that were filtering through the Pyrenees (1789–1808); the country, devastated by the fight against the French invaders (1808–1814) – what in England is called the Peninsular War – and subsequently governed by a fierce and unrepentant reactionary faction (1814–1833, with a three-year interruption), could provide no encouragement for the development of speculative thought. The universities dispensed second-hand information, the Academies languished in indifference and routine activity, the nascent periodical press was effectively muzzled, there was severe censorship of foreign books, and Spanish presses offered almost nothing capable of exercising the mind. It was only after the death of Ferdinand VII (1833) that intellectuals and writers began to breathe freely; not very freely, to be sure, but enough to give grounds for hope that the unhappy period just ended would not be repeated. It was then that desire for change and improvement became concentrated on literature, which had acquired new vitality with the Romantic movement that belatedly entered the country with the return of the exiles who had fled during Fernando's reign.

We need to emphasize the accessory function of literature during the first half of the nineteenth century in Spain, and especially during the Romantic period. Thought, in its broadest sense – ideas, beliefs, opinions, intuitions – was most often to be found in lyric poetry, in drama, and especially in critical essays often disguised as 'local color'. Obviously there was nothing consistent or particularly logical about this; but it showed at least that writers' brains were beginning to work again after a long fallow period, that writers' eyes were taking a sharp look at the contemporary scene, and that writers' pens were being wielded in response to timid hopes of national progress and rehabilitation. However, the country's political, social, and economic condition was far from hopeful. The death of Ferdinand VII opened a period of civil strife between *Carlistas*, supporters of Ferdinand's brother Don Carlos, and *Isabelinos*, those who favored Doña Isabella, the dead king's daughter, who had acceded to the throne thanks to her father's revocation of the Salic law excluding women from the succession. In very general terms, it was the Carlists who wished to perpetuate the old régime: political absolutism, traditional institutions, religious intolerance, preference for an agricultural and grazing economy; their chief strength lay in the rural and semi-rural areas of the north and northeast of Spain. Among Isabella's partisans were the liberals, those who favored representative government, tolerance in questions of religion, and an industrial and commercial economy; their strength was based largely in the cities and, in general, in the country's central and southern regions. The Carlist cause, represented either in the person of Don Carlos or those of his successors as pretenders to the Spanish throne, led to an outbreak of hostilities several times during the course of Isabella II's reign (1833–1868), and a lasting peace was not achieved until 1876. The threat of war, either real or latent, gave a strongly military stamp to Queen Isabella's governments, and the ambitions of certain army generals led to *pronunciamientos* or political pressures in which the sovereign herself often played a leading role. The intrigues of Isabella's court, the perversion of the political process by corrupt royal favorites and insubordinate military men, the queen's personal immorality, all eventually exhausted the liberal faction's initial sympathies toward the queen; they had hoped that her accession to the throne would inaugurate a splendid epoch in her country's history, like that it had experienced under the first Queen Isabella.

And so the Krausist movement, with which this book deals, took root in a climate of disappointed hopes; and the young men who, beginning in 1854, received the teachings of the school's founder, Julián Sanz del Río, were those who felt the disappointment most keenly. The wretched reality they saw around them led them to draw away from it as one draws away from a source of infection, and this withdrawal soon revealed their small numbers. At first there were very few of them, but for this very reason they felt closely linked to each other, huddled together like an aloof, austere little band of brothers. Later, encouraged by their teacher, they were to discover that their task was to *think*, and that thinking is a hard job that demands, in addition to a lofty sense of dedication, large stores of effort and will. *Reason* was to be their instrument and guide, in the dual sense, active and passive, of which I spoke above. They were, in short, the men who constituted an intellectual *class* for the first time in Spain, a 'thinking minority' as they called themselves, a 'horde of fanatical sectarians' as their enemies preferred to call them, using the phrase of a well-known traditionalist.

A possible linkage has been suggested between the Krausist movement and the Revolution of September, 1868, which resulted in Isabella's exile and was followed by a six-year period of instability during which Spain tried, in quick succession, a Provisional Government (1868–1870), a new dynasty with Amadeo of Savoy as king (1870–1873), a Republic that soon dissolved into anarchy (1873), and a military *coup d'état* that opened the way for a Bourbon restoration (1874) in the person of Alfonso XII, son of the dethroned Isabella. It must be noted, however, that if by 'linkage' a causal connection is implied between Krausism and revolution, the suggestion has no basis in fact. In 1868 those who opposed Isabella's monarchy were legion, and the immense majority had never heard either of Krausism or Krausists. Strictly speaking, the Revolution of 1868 was a military *pronunciamiento* engineered by the same generals who had been dancing attendance on the queen for years, receiving her favors or her slights according to circumstances and the royal whim. But on this occasion, no doubt eager to acquire prestige and to place civilian talent at the service of plans for reform, the officers who had taken part in the coup made considerable efforts to attract the 'thinking minority' that was emerging from the universities or taught in them; and of course the Krausists formed a strong element in this group.

Hence it is not surprising that during the six-year revolutionary period the Krausists – along with others who, although they were not Krausists, sympathized with one aspect or another of the school – gained a solid foothold not only in centers of instruction, as was only to be expected, but also in various departments of governmental administration. They were experts at drawing up suggestions, plans, and projects, and their contribution was more doctrinal than practical. In the University of Madrid the rector, Fernando de Castro, a prominent Krausist, pondered a plan for university reform. In the presidency of the Republic Nicolás Salmerón, another well-known Krausist, advocated a federalized Spain that would put an end to political and social discord. Other more or less enthusiastic Krausists worked on the text of the Constitution of 1869 and on plans for the Ministry of Finance, public works, charitable institutions, public education, and the like. But disenchantment with the Revolution spread quickly among the 'thinking minority'. Their eyes fixed on a lofty ideal, their souls filled with utopian zeal, the Krausists soon lost patience with the skepticism – if not stubborn opposition – with which the real world greeted their efforts. It might be said that they were condemned to live in a state of perpetual frustration, consoled only by the hope, which grew frailer day by day, that the future would prove them right.

But the future – at least the immediate future – did not treat them gently. Restoration of the Bourbon monarchy brought with it a reaction against the doctrines and ideologies that had fed the revolutionary movement, and Krausist philosophy was one of these. Some of the school's most conspicuous representatives in the world of education were expelled from their chairs and exiled to various points on the country's periphery. The school, as such, had received a mortal wound. And as the ties that had bound its members together were loosened, their faith in the speedy arrival of a better world defrauded, they gradually moved toward other modes of thought which, though retaining a fundamental idealism, seemed more in tune with the here and now. A happy combination of noble aspiration and practical common sense would, however, place an unmistakable imprint on their later contributions to the fields of pedagogy, law, sociology, and aesthetics. But a study of this phase of Krausism's later influence lies outside the scope of the present book.

J. L.-M.

Madrid, July 1979

Preface to the first Spanish edition

About the middle of the last century there appeared in Spain's cultural
life the initial phase of an ideological change which would lead, in the
decades that followed, to a shift in the viewpoint from which Spaniards
examined their material and spiritual contributions in the past and tried
to anticipate the trajectory of their future activities. As a partial justification of this study, let me begin by saying that not a few of the
consequences of that shift in attitude are very much in existence today;
and this makes the task of finding and defining them still more difficult.
Indeed, anyone who confronts as a spectator the life of his time, or an
immediately past time, is overwhelmed by the quantity of information
that pours in upon him. Lack of perspective gives him a deceptive view
of things, in which, at the outset, both the substantial and the accidental
claim the same measure of careful attention. But in addition he feels
disturbed by the suspicion that when he pins down and interprets the
ideas, beliefs, and passions of his contemporaries, what he is really
doing is to define and justify his own ideas, beliefs, and passions by
objectifying them. He wants to be an impartial spectator yet feels, willy-
nilly, the impulse to participate in the drama that unfolds before his
eyes. Chained to the moment in which he himself lives, he cannot draw
away from it to view it as a reality from which he has consciously
detached himself, and can contemplate from a number of viewpoints.
And yet such detachment is indispensable, even though it may be
illusory.

Some of the aspects of Spain's intellectual history offered in these
pages have been in their time – and in some cases still are – subjects of
bitter controversy, and for this very reason the object of very contradictory judgments. Often the passion aroused by the ideological disputes that Krausism brought with it seems to derive from a transfer to
the intellectual plane of the impassioned feelings natural to a country
torn by civil strife for a half a century. Under the troubled surface of
nineteenth-century Spain I have tried to discover some elements which,
I believe, characterize the second half of that century within the history
of ideas. As with any other period, this one too tempts me to set down

what was potential in it and what was real, what it might have been and what it in fact was. For we must not forget that it was a period over which a question mark still hovers. During it, problems were made flesh and constantly tormented those who most prided themselves on calmness and serenity. The almost frantic vehemence with which the most bizarre theories were postulated makes us suspect that fundamentally we are dealing with a defensive attitude, a challenge born of deep-seated uncertainty and nourished by a desire to steer an ideal course through an inconstant and elusive world.

The Spaniard of the mid-nineteenth century felt a vague dissatisfaction within himself which gradually spread and darkened his whole sphere of activity. Inwardly, he felt relegated to a humble corner of the modern European scene, from which he watched, with an avidity not unmixed with mortification, the more relevant role played by other actors not of his blood. It was then, during that twenty-year span which preceded and followed the Bourbon restoration, that three polemical attitudes appeared on which judgment of Spain's cultural history would be based for years to come. The first of these attitudes embodied the opinion – latent ever since the eighteenth century – that the Spanish genius, eminent in the intuitive grasp of inner and outer reality, in the poetic vision of God, the world, and man, was incapable of abstract reasoning, minute observation, and patient experimentation; incapable, in short, of philosophy and science. Imaginative exuberance, bursts of passion, all-absorbing individualism, lack of intimacy, were considered to be special traits of the Spanish genius. All of them had contributed toward giving an eruptive and spasmodic stamp to the culture that had sprung from that genius – 'orgiastic', Ortega y Gasset was to say later; Unamuno would call it 'African'. The second attitude was that of persons who, without accepting this diagnosis but recognizing that the current cultural inadequacy was indisputable, examined Spain's history seeking the point at which that history had 'changed course' under the pressure of specific factors, had betrayed itself, as it were, and destroyed the cultural structure that Spain had been building, until then, in collaboration with other Western nations. To the psychological interpretation of the first attitude, the second opposed a determinist interpretation founded on the constricting action of outside elements. The Inquisition, the Counter-Reformation, Habsburg absolutism, taken separately or together, had been the disturbing elements of Spain's cultural configuration. The sixteenth century had witnessed this unfortunate deviation. And lastly, the third attitude was that held by persons who insisted that not Spain but Protestant Europe had broken the spiritual unity, and with it the sense of cultural community, that had been achieved during the Middle Ages. They justified sixteenth- and seventeenth-century Spanish intransigence as a logical result of the noble, though fruitless, attempt to restore that broken unity. This last group identified Spanish culture with Catholicism to the point of considering as anti-Spanish any ideological current that tended to undermine the Church's sovereignty, and as an aberration any spiritual manifestation tinged with heterodoxy.

Underlying this dissatisfaction was the undeniable fact of Spain's material backwardness. The Spaniard who crossed the Pyrenees was forced to recognize, no matter how inflexible his national pride, that in the sphere of material things his country lagged far behind the rest of Western Europe. The mere evidence of that disparity was in itself a cause for discouragement; but it was a still greater cause in a period when the material level of life was viewed as the index of a culture's degree of vigor and efficiency. A bourgeoisie conscious of its mission of renewal, of its increasing command over the obstacles of the physical surroundings, inclined to read history as a chronicle of man's irresistible progress toward a fuller life, smiled complacently upon the multitude of material creations which made possible, as well as justified, the extent of its power. The bourgeoisie, newly arrived at full enjoyment of the purely normative and ideal values of traditional culture, had ended by appropriating them, immediately placing them at the service of utilitarian ends. The eighteenth-century Enlightenment, an aspiration to spiritual improvement, had been replaced by Progress, an aspiration to material betterment. Culture became a simple dimension of Progress, and often the two terms were assigned the same meaning.

The Spaniard of the mid-nineteenth century, unaware of the error implicit in so pragmatic an interpretation of culture, was dazzled by the results that material progress had brought to other European countries. If he had possessed an adequate notion of his own spiritual heritage, a notion kept strictly separate both from patriotic effusion and facile criticism, he might perhaps have been able to judge with minimal accuracy the meaning of the change that had recently taken place in the Western European spirit. But in reality he did not possess this knowledge, and the fact that he did not shows through the intellectual fumblings, the frequent diatribes, and the violence itself of the period's controversies. In trying to shorten the distance between his country and the rest of Europe, his lack of reliable criteria caused him to favor men or ideas that had received only fleeting attention. Convinced heart and soul that he was hopelessly behind the times, this conviction impelled him, as a strong psychological reaction, to idolize everything new. The important thing was to be in the latest fashion, to cut one's ideas according to the most recent pattern. A scientific hypothesis, a philosophical doctrine, a style of art, embraced with blind enthusiasm, was abandoned as soon as the suspicion arose that it had been replaced by others in the interest of cultured Europe. The educated Spaniard had never had so unbounded a zeal for the fortuitous. A man like Manuel de la Revilla, whose intelligence was sharp and his culture extensive, was able, in the course of a life lasting only thirty-five years, to militate successively in the ranks of Krausism, neo-Kantianism, and positivism. The best-known reviews of the period display a constant and fervent desire for modernity. The translator's pen moved tirelessly to place within the Spanish reader's grasp articles and essays that reflected, or aspired to reflect, the *current state* of the different provinces of knowledge. And partisans of the dominant philosophical system – Krausism – called it, by definition, *the brand-new philosophy*.

It was indeed a mistaken perspective, a result of the suffocating isolation in which the Spanish intellect had lived for so long. And yet we must excuse it because, however mistaken, it represented the initial phase of the fruitful spiritual change that was to appear in subsequent decades. The errors of that perspective could be corrected, as in fact they were later. They were errors of focus, distortions caused by the rapid overview of a visual field that had suddenly and unexpectedly expanded. The cultured Spaniard of those days was in large measure self-taught. What he learned, whether well or badly, had a strong adventitious flavor. His intellectual hunger, innocent of all critical refinement, fed on thoroughly seasoned as well as tasteless victuals. In the end, what saved him from ideological indigestion was a basic integrity, a clear ethical intuition which tended to personalize the most abstract questions, to fit them into the frame of moral conscience; that is, to turn them into very necessary tasks of the human condition. In Krause first, as later in Schopenhauer, Nietzsche, and Bergson, this inquisitive and capricious Spaniard sought above all else a means of allaying his ethical unrest. From Sanz del Río to Ortega, from Fernando de Castro to Unamuno, from Francisco Giner to Antonio Machado, this concern is always unmistakable, the result of an instinctive grasp of the fact that man is more important than ideas. And it is interesting to note how, at the precise moment when the Spaniard is most eager to be primarily intellectual, the frustration of that eagerness shows that he possesses a rich potential of human qualities – reveals, in short, man himself in all his greatness and misery.

This study will attempt to draw the outlines of Spanish Krausism, a spiritual movement to which – though more out of laziness of mind than serious thought – has been attributed Spain's incorporation into modern European thought. The Europeanization of Spain is far from being a recent concern. It arises, already vociferous, in the eighteenth century; it persists, though concealed by more peremptory concerns, during the first half of the nineteenth; and it finds at last, in the doctrine imported by Julián Sanz del Río, the opportunity to be structured into a militant school. And so Krausism's 'newness' lies not so much in advocating the Europeanization of Spain as in identifying Europe with the rational view of the world and, in conformity with that identification, in trying to guide Spanish culture in the direction of rationalism. I freely confess that what attracts me is the characterization of a cultural mode rather than the analysis of a philosophical system. What a certain type of Spaniard tried to see in Krausism is much more significant for me than what Krause put into his doctrine, or what Sanz del Río was trying to accomplish by importing it. I also believe that I should limit myself to describing the phase in which this spiritual movement appears in its greatest degree of homogeneity, namely during the years between the Revolution of 1854 and the early days of the Restoration. It is true that Krausism survived for a long time after this second chronological landmark, either as a doctrinal ingredient in disciplines like pedagogy, sociology, law, etc., or as an ethical ingredient in writers like Galdós, Clarín, Antonio Machado, and a few others. But it is not Krausism as a survival, but as a living doctrine, which interests me here.

First of all I wish to thank the John Simon Guggenheim Memorial Foundation which, by granting me a fellowship in 1950–1951, made this study possible; the librarians of the Hemeroteca Municipal, the Biblioteca Nacional, and the Ateneo, of Madrid; those of the Bibliothèque Nationale of Paris and the British Museum of London; and my colleagues Professor William L. Fichter, Professor Albert J. Salvan, and Dr José Amor y Vázquez, of Brown University, who have patiently read the manuscript.

J. L.-M.

Brown University
Providence, Rhode Island, U.S.A.

Note to the second Spanish edition

The first edition of this book went out of print nearly ten years ago. Since then I have inclined to believe that my purpose in writing it had been accomplished: namely, that of investigating and casting light on a movement of ideas very frequently spoken of but almost never clearly defined. I think I can say without exaggeration that the book did indeed carry out this task. Its vicissitudes, nonetheless, are not lacking in interest. For a number of years after its publication in Mexico in 1956 it could not be sold openly in Spain, and it was the object of clandestine traffic by Spaniards traveling abroad or foreigners entering the country. Copies were made of a number of chapters – I have seen some of these in manuscript – which passed from hand to hand, especially among university students. The book has also served as a stimulus to other scholars interested in the Spanish Krausist movement.

I have good reason to believe that the book is still sought and read with interest, and many people have urged me to have it reprinted. The result is this new edition. I have not wished, however, to write a new book, in which I would have had to take into account the large number of studies on Krausism published during the last twenty years. That would have been an undertaking too great for my energies and far removed from my present concerns. Hence I have confined myself to adding certain indispensable bibliographical material, in particular other studies of mine written since 1956 in which I tried to expand or explain aspects of the book that clearly required such treatment. These references, and a careful correction of obvious *errata*, have sufficed to complete this elementary revision.

University of Texas
Austin

I

Julián Sanz del Río

1. The good tidings

In the history of nineteenth-century Spanish thought there is one moment that deserves special attention: it is the moment when Julián Sanz del Río, holder of the chair of History of Philosophy at the University of Madrid, rose to deliver the inaugural address of the 1857–1858 academic year.[1] Far from being the conventional homily that might have been expected on such an occasion, his *Discurso* sketched out an entire program for the articulation of human knowledge, a vast projection into the pedagogical sphere of a philosophy that aspired to a state of universal harmony. The speaker envisaged a university, a sort of *Civitas Scientiae*, where all the multiple activities of the intellect would flow together, and from which, once their union had taken place, they would flow out again to enrich the spiritual seedbed of all humanity. It is hardly necessary to state that the university of which he spoke was an abstract one which, 'as the worthy abode of a divine idea', could prudently be located in the unattainable sphere of utopia. Using the words of his old friend and fellow student Henri-Frédéric Amiel, Sanz del Río might have said that 'the Ideal poisoned for him all imperfect possessions'. As a utopia, the university envisioned by Sanz del Río attempted to evade immediate and distasteful reality. The new organization would be the sanctuary where worship would be offered to the future 'ideal of humanity', and where the men who were adepts of the new doctrine – namely, the *harmonic rationalism* of Karl Christian Friedrich Krause (1781–1832) – would carry out their priestly mission.

It may seem an exaggeration to compare the Spanish branch of Krausist philosophy to a religious cult, but in fact Sanz del Río himself offers a basis for such a comparison in a number of places in his *Discurso*. After sketching with broad strokes the structure of Krausist doctrine, the speaker admonishes the members of the university

I

community who are listening to him, 'Once raised to this spiritual priest-hood...it will be your primary duty to teach the truth, to propagate it and live wholly for it...You must honor your teaching with the witness of your conduct and defend it as the religion of your calling, under the Religion that unites us all.'[2] Possession and teaching of the truth, metaphysics and pedagogy, priesthood and proselytizing: in the *Discurso*, which is Sanz del Río's first philosophical publication, the dual aspect into which the activities of the Spanish Krausist movement were divided is already apparent. Indeed, it is the preface that antici-pates by three years the appearance of *Ideal de la Humanidad para la vida* (1860), a work in which, by adapting Krause's *Urbild der Menschheit* (1811), the Spanish thinker endowed the budding move-ment with a code of doctrine and conduct.[3] Sanz del Río's later writings merely elaborate the conceptual outline drawn up in the *Discurso*, an elaboration that was only partial, for the leader of the Spanish Krausist school could not, for a number of reasons, accomplish more than a pre-liminary task of ideological transplantation. It was his followers who developed the Krausist movement's intellectual program, exploring with the aid of the new doctrinal instrument the domains of philosophy, law, history, pedagogy, religion, and the social sciences.

But a master, a body of doctrine, and a group of disciples are not sufficient reason to confer on the Krausist school the attributes of a religious cult, nor would the fact that it also gave rise to spectacular conversions, heresies, apostasies, and persecutions. Other philosophical sects display similar vicissitudes in the course of their evolution. What is really remarkable about the Krausist movement, in contrast to other philosophical systems which consider philosophy as something more than a mere adjunct to theology, lies in the profound religious spirit that informs all its doctrines, its metaphysics as well as its ethics, its aesthetics as well as its philosophy of history. Krausism has often been defined as a systematic theosophy. And indeed, unless an effort is made to dig into the system's theosophic subsoil, we will reach the mistaken conclusion that it is an empty metaphysical construction, like so many that arose under the influence of Kantian criticism. But the fact is that a very strong current of religious concern flowed from the doctrine to its sup-porters and aroused in them the sense of a very pressing mission whose ultimate goal was universal brotherhood, a new *ideal* of humanity according to which humanity is thought of as 'a collective person in unity of idea and purpose, and of constructive work toward that purpose'.[4] Such were the 'good tidings' preached by Sanz del Río on the occasion we have just described. Reading between the lines of this convoluted and wordy *Discurso*, we can discern the pattern that the Spanish Krausist movement means to follow in its struggle to bring about the new order of things. This pattern includes the following postulates: (a) a definition of the content and method of scientific knowledge; (b) a new vision of man as synthesis of the universe; and (c) a harmonic organization of humanity. But the objectives set by the speaker in presenting his doctrine are not reduced to these three alone. Krausism is not simply an epistemology, a philosophical anthropology, and a philosophy of history. It is a systematic philosophy, or attempts to be one, in which the different facets of the real can be accommodated and harmonized. But, in addition, at the very heart of the system beats a reforming and humanitarian impulse that translates into a program of action substantially similar to those expressed at about the same time in the social philosophy advocated by such men as Fourier and Saint-Simon. This activism, whose roots are to be found in the Enlightenment of the eighteenth century, appears frequently in the nineteenth with whiffs of messianic inspiration. As a result of the positivist view of history, or under the influence of Hegelian philosophy, all of Europe heard the echoes of some social panacea or other.[5] Krause was, therefore, very much a man of his time in proclaiming that, after a long period of confusion, humanity was about to cross the threshold of full maturity. But the German philosopher added an intensely personal touch by identifying the ideal of political and social perfection with that of religious fulfillment. The advent of the better world would result from a rational grasp of the idea of God and of divine order. In this respect it should be pointed out that Krause revitalized the tradition originating in the fourteenth-century German mystics. Up to a point, his philosophy can be considered as the rational extension of the mysticism of men like Heinrich Suso, Johannes Tauler, and especially Master Eckhart. To the ingenuous pantheism of these men was closely linked a desire for social concord built on a foundation of Christian ethics. Their respective aspirations could be summarized, in Eckhart's words, by the establishment of a society in which men would live 'in such a way that virtue would no longer be an effort'.

2. Years of apprenticeship

The circumstances that had determined Julián Sanz del Río's philosophical mission seem fortuitous at first glance. It might be said that an inconstant star had guided this introverted and austere Castilian from the moment when he emerged as a Doctor of Canon Law from the University of Granada in 1836 to that other moment in 1867 when, having drawn the fire of the reactionary faction, he was stripped of his university chair by arbitrary decree of one of Isabella II's ministers. His professional life, therefore, coincided with the reign of Isabella II, during which Spanish life, in the absence of solider virtues, had to settle for making a virtue of improvisation. In 1837, after a previous and abortive attempt in 1822, the University of Madrid was improvised with the few assets – not all of them useless – brought from the decrepit University of Alcalá de Henares. In 1845 Pedro José Pidal improvised a 'modern' plan of studies for higher education, using the French university system as a model. In 1852 an improvised Faculty of Philosophy was given university status. By means of the quick and easy procedure known as 'a stroke of the pen', the youth of Spain was to be given suitable instruments for intellectual work. Reforms and counter-reforms followed hard on each other's heels, and the rapidity with which they took place was itself an indication of their pitifully small positive content. Most of them had been conceived by politicians playing at pedagogy, and reflected the exquisite vacuity that lurked under the rhetorical flourishes of the period's political life. They were not really plans for university studies, but plans of study that might perhaps have been useful had university studies in fact existed. But there were none. There were no competent professors, no libraries, no laboratories.

No one thought of studying... Instruction was pure farce, a tacit agreement between teachers and pupils founded on mutual ignorance, slovenliness, and almost criminal neglect. The experimental sciences had been forgotten; physics was studied without ever seeing a machine or a piece of apparatus... If anything was left of the old order of things it was lack of discipline, disorder, the bribery involved in voting and the provision of chairs by examination.[6]

It was indeed a sorry picture, made still more lamentable by the hypocrisy and irresponsibility of official pedagogues. With the possible exception of jurists and theologians, there was scarcely anyone competent to perform the teaching work that the reformers of public instruction were supposedly trying to carry out. Under such circumstances it is not strange that someone had the idea of improvising a body of professors charged with the dual task of teaching the youth of university age as well as preparing future occupants of chairs. And in fact Pedro Gómez de la Serna, Minister of the Interior during the last government of Espartero's regency, appointed Julián Sanz del Río, by a decree of 8 June 1843, interim professor of philosophy at the newly established University of Madrid, under the express condition that the appointee spend two years in Germany perfecting his philosophical knowledge in the 'chief schools' there.

Sanz del Río's philosophical baggage before his trip to Germany is a matter for conjecture, but there is no question that it was not excessive. Until then his academic and professional career had been confined to the area of civil and canon law, and, in view of the way the study of law was understood in Spain at the time, it is doubtful that the future professor could have extracted from it any nourishment for his metaphysical concerns. Before 1843 his knowledge of German philosophy had been indirect and desultory. His German was very imperfect, as can be inferred from his own statements.[7] He may have had no other information about the post-Kantian idealist philosophers than that which could be found – in vague and distorted form – in the eclecticism of Victor Cousin and the spiritualism of Royer-Collard. A short time before he became the vigorous and unquestioning exponent of Krausist ideas, his only knowledge of Krausist philosophy had come from reading the *Cours de Droit naturel* by the German jurist Heinrich Ahrens, who taught, from his chair at the University of Brussels, a system of philosophy of law directly inspired by Krause's doctrines. Ahrens's book was translated into Spanish by a friend and colleague of Sanz del Río, Ruperto Navarro Zamorano, and successive generations of Spanish and Hispano-American jurists have profited from this Spanish version published in 1841 and reprinted many times. But his first contact with Krausism, though superficial and confused, seems to have aroused in Sanz del Río an interest bordering on obsession. Krause's progressivist and humanitarian ethics served as the back door through which the budding philosopher slipped into the labyrinth of the 'brand-new philosophy'. The 'chief schools' which he was supposed to study in Germany, according to the terms of his appointment, were reduced to one: harmonic rationalism. And this exclusiveness, openly dogmatic in nature, was to give direction for several decades not only to speculative studies but to the whole intellectual renascence in Spain.

Paris represented the first stage on this journey in search of philosophical adventures. Victor Cousin's eclectic spiritualism, offspring of a *mariage de convenance* between the Scottish school and post-Kantian transcendentalism, had been officially accepted and held sway in the

French capital. This brilliant and innocuous philosophy responded to the laudable desire to harmonize the most widely disparate doctrines in a spirit very characteristic of the times, which had also inspired the reigning July Monarchy – a monarchy also anxious to reconcile the irreconcilable. In Paris Sanz del Río had an interview with the high priest of French philosophy, and his impression both of the philosopher and the philosophy is tinged with a good deal of scorn:

[Philosophy] as a pure science and an independent science is not cultivated with any degree of profundity or sincerity; people work in philosophy, but subordinating it to an end which is not philosophy but rather...politics, social reform, and even purposes that are hardly noble, such as vanity... I visited Monsieur Cousin and, though I would not dream of judging him as a man, I will say that as a philosopher he contrived to lower even the rather poor opinion in which I held him. I regret more every day the influence that French philosophy and science – a science of imposture and pure appearance – have exercised among us for more than half a century. What has it brought us except a disinclination to work for ourselves, false knowledge, and especially immorality and petulant egotism?[8]

The pervasiveness of Sanz del Rio's aversion cannot be exaggerated. To begin with, it is very unusual for a cultivated Spaniard of the period to condemn forms of a foreign culture which had been nourishing the thought of his own country for a long time. It is true that ever since the early years of the eighteenth century there had been repeated outcries against the abject imitation of everything originating in France, but they were not accompanied by censure of French cultural values. They were more likely to be complaints arising out of an injured sense of patriotism or, more precisely, out of fear of losing by foreign invasion everything deemed essential for the existence and persistence of the national genius. The disdain shown by Sanz del Río toward French philosophy – and which is only a symptom of a generalized scorn for everything French – responds to reasons of a very different kind. Against xenophobes and cultural nationalists the standard-bearer of the Spanish Krausist movement would always insist on the need to go beyond Spain's borders in search of stimuli for his country's spiritual rejuvenation, convinced as he was that any authentic renascence is – as Azorín was to say later – the fecundation of national thought by foreign thought. But he was to deny vehemently that such stimuli could be found in a culture like the French, which besides being incompatible with the Spanish spirit also threatened to destroy the ethical bases on which that future renascence would necessarily have to be built.[9]

Considerably more profitable was the visit made by Sanz del Río in the summer of 1843 to Heinrich Ahrens in Brussels, a visit no doubt motivated by the enthusiasm he had felt on reading the *Cours de Droit naturel*. His determination to dedicate himself entirely to the study of Krausist philosophy, with the ostensible aim of using it as a means to judge the suitability of other doctrines for teaching purposes which might interest the Spanish government, dates from his visit to Brussels. The summary aversion with which he regarded French philosophy, and the indifference he was later to exhibit, in Germany, for any doctrine but Krause's, make us suspect that when he proposed to go abroad he was chiefly guided by the desire to examine at close quarters a form of speculative thought that he already considered to be the only one worthy of study and admiration. In this respect it must be admitted that he did not carry out faithfully the official mission on which he had been sent.

If due note is taken of his obsessive preference for Krausism, the significance for Sanz del Río of his interviews with Ahrens is understandable. The German jurist had studied under Krause in Göttingen before 1831, the year when both professor and pupil had had to flee from that university center, where at the time a deeply suspicious intolerance was attempting to smother any attempt at ideological non-conformity.[10] It was Ahrens who, impressed by the Spanish student's neophyte zeal, suggested to Sanz del Río the idea of settling in Heidelberg, where two of Krause's distinguished disciples were teaching: Baron Hermann von Leonhardi, the master's son-in-law and editor, and Carl David August Röder, interested, like Ahrens, in the philosophy of law. Sanz del Río worked with both men from the autumn of 1843 to the end of 1844. In Heidelberg he lodged as a pupil in the home of the historian Georg Weber, whose *Allgemeine Weltgeschichte* he was to translate into Spanish years later.[11] And as a fellow pupil he had a young man from Geneva who was also much given at that time to the study of Krausist philosophy: Henri-Frédéric Amiel.

3. Teaching career

After his return to Madrid in 1844 Sanz del Río modestly declined to occupy the chair of philosophy he had been offered, claiming that his professional preparation was still too deficient to allow him to confront the responsibilities of university teaching. And to correct this deficiency he spent ten years in retirement in the town of Illescas, systematically rethinking and patiently reworking Krause's philosophy. At last, in

1854, he returned to academic tasks. His innate shyness and a certain puritanical austerity of word and gesture gradually dissipated over the course of years, in the warmth of his hearers' enthusiasm. Professors, literary men, and political figures abounded among the students who crowded his classroom, where, for the first time in Madrid, glimpses were offered of faraway ideological horizons and new methods of study and work were contrived with remarkable discipline and enthusiasm. Sanz del Río's influence was extraordinary from 1857 until his death in 1869, a period that witnessed the emergence of the first generation of Spanish Krausists. In greater or lesser degree these men were spurred by the desire to break down the wall of provincial distrust which, by isolating Spain from European thought, had condemned the country to spiritual apathy and material penury. But their contemplation of con- temporary Spain – ignorant and garrulous, indigent and bleeding from many wounds – also made them feel the need of breaking with the Spain of the past, the Spain that had arisen from the Counter-Reforma- tion and buttressed Catholic imperialism, the Spain that was both militaristic and priest-ridden and which, rightly or wrongly, they held responsible for the miseries of the moment. Received ideas, traditional beliefs, tiresome clichés, and the trivialities of the cultural nationalism then in vogue were of no avail in this task of carrying out a historical 'purification'. According to the views of this generation, it was essential to fight under any ideological banner whatever so long as it was radically new and offered at least a faint hope of rescuing the country from its prevailing spiritual atrophy. It is useless to repeat, as has been done so many times, that Krausist philosophy was not the solution, that when Sanz del Río went to seek enlightenment he merely got entangled in the metaphysical web spun by a German philosopher who even today is unknown to most of his countrymen. Menéndez Pelayo's inventory of the Krausist movement, which he describes as 'a horde of fanatical sectarians...a sort of Masonic lodge, a mutual aid society, a tribe, a circle of *illuminati*, a clique...something, in short, murky and repug- nant to every independent soul',[12] would no doubt be plausible if it were accompanied by an explanation of how such a sinister alliance could seduce men whose rectitude and independence of judgment were unquestionable even at the time. In the absence of such an explanation, Menéndez Pelayo's invective must be relegated to the barren terrain of overblown rhetoric. For it was not enough to lament the scorn shown by the inquisitive and dissatisfied young men of the time toward the cultural values of the Spain of the past, nor could these lost sheep be brought back to 'true knowledge' and 'sound philosophy' merely by setting the critical bibliography of *La ciencia española* under their noses. Neither suggestions of a return to Luis Vives's 'criticism' or Fox Morcillo's 'harmonism', nor impressive lists of authors and works that reflected the Spanish cultural past could produce the desired effect at a moment whose chief characteristics were lack of appreciation – no doubt largely unfounded – for that past, and a new feeling of perplexity about the future. Even Juan Valera, who always maintained an equal distance between ingenuous praise of things Spanish and idolatrous admiration for things foreign, revealed the gnawing dismay felt at the time by those who most prided themselves on their moderation and equanimity. 'I venture to say that in the last fifty or sixty years', he wrote in 1868, 'it seems we are worse off than ever... The important thing now is not to praise ourselves in public, nor to boast about what we were, but to point out our own faults.'[13]

This was the state of uneasiness which was largely responsible for Sanz del Río's success; he, for his part, though he could not hope to set it at rest, did succeed in bringing it to the surface and placing it in a setting where it could have positive results. For a metaphysical anxiety lay at the core of that uneasiness, and this in its turn usually carries the promise of an intellectual flowering. Like all genuine teachers, Sanz del Río was essentially an *accoucheur* of ideas. The young men who listened to him, often without quite understanding him, were distressed as much by the difficulty of diagnosing their own unrest as by their desire to give form to the flashes of thought evoked by their teacher's words. The very abstruseness of an unfamiliar and technical philosophical language, the tortuous clauses vibrating with intractable echoes of German syntax, the demonstrations *more geometrico*, were so many challenges to the listener's timid curiosity, to his mental stamina, and at the very least aroused the perplexity that is the threshold of speculative thought. To begin with, these young men learned that it is not easy to make philosophy, and that the difficulty of making philosophy was practically insuperable in a cultural setting that had remained almost entirely isolated from modern philosophy. In philosophical matters – and to this degree Menéndez Pelayo was right – Spanish thought had yielded its most mature fruits in the sixteenth century. But of essentially new philosophy, the philosophy that began with Descartes, almost nothing was known, and even if something had been it is doubtful whether the seeds of that knowledge would have taken root in the subsoil of Spain, so long barren of intellectual rigor and discipline. Sanz del Río and his followers were the first to immerse the Spanish mind in modern rationalism. Had they done no more than this the cultural scope of their work would have been considerable, for understanding European culture means, in large measure, understanding the cultural forms assumed by that rationalism. To accept or reject Europe – as Unamuno later realized – meant accepting or rejecting the rationalist world-view that had reigned supreme ever since the seventeenth century. All the rest meant putting the cart before the horse, mistaking the accidents – the objective forms of culture – for the substance, the primacy of reason over the other faculties of the psyche. Compared with the attempts at Europeanization which had begun in Spain in the eighteenth century, the Krausist movement was the first to see clearly to the root of the problem. The others had contented themselves with advocating the adoption of foreign ways of thinking and acting; that is, political ideas, economic doctrines, social practices, literary forms, styles in art, without realizing that such ways were organic manifestations of a certain attitude toward life which – fortunately or unfortunately, for the moment it does not matter which – was unknown in Spain. If advocacy of a Europeanized Spain is accepted, the conclusion will have to be that the Krausists viewed the problem more logically than their predecessors. It was not isolated forms of European culture that they were eager to transfer to the Spanish side of the Pyrenees. It was the rational interpretation of the world that fed those forms. For, as Sanz del Río proclaimed, 'such is the force of reason... [that] either alone or in company, favored or persecuted, time has no power over her; each new word of hers opens a new horizon, extends and affirms, after great struggles, the realm of truth'.[14]

2

Harmonic rationalism

1. Position in the history of philosophy

Historians of philosophy place Krause's doctrine within the cycle of systems that claim the exclusive right to be heirs of Kant. Like Fichte, Schelling, Hegel, Reinhold, and so many others, Krause lays claim to the title of sole true exponent of the master of Königsberg, and as such considers himself better equipped than anyone else to explain and refine Kantian criticism. He treats Fichte, Hegel, and especially Schelling with open hostility. They were the fashionable philosophers, *Universitätsphilosophen* as Schopenhauer disdainfully called them, who fought shamelessly for official favor and tried to monopolize the most desirable university chairs in Germany for themselves and their followers. Berlin, Jena, Göttingen, Heidelberg, and Munich were the intellectual centers from which post-Kantian idealism spread most vigorously. But Krause's animosity toward his colleagues was more personal than doctrinal. In the strictly philosophical sphere his thought was enriched and polished by contact with other systems which, though very different from his in content, displayed striking similarities as to method. Unmistakable traces of other contemporary doctrines can often be found in Krausist philosophy. There is nothing surprising about this if it is remembered that the philosophers who shared the Kantian inheritance constructed their metaphysical castles, in part at least, by borrowing ideas from other contemporary thinkers. The point of departure is usually the same: elaboration of part of a pre-existing system. And from this inconspicuous beginning a new theory gradually emerges which is brazenly assigned the role of supplanting the parent doctrine. This is Fichte's position with respect to Kant, Schelling's with respect to Fichte, Hegel's with respect to Schelling. It is also the position of Krause, who believed that his doctrine had achieved the much-desired and necessary reconciliation between the subjective idealism of Kant and Fichte and the absolute idealism of Schelling and Hegel. Kant's analytics, Fichte's reformist and humanitarian aspirations, Schelling's pantheism, and Hegel's system of ultimate universal notions – categories – all manage to fit, with lesser or greater modifications, into harmonic rationalism.[1]

2. Analytics

Krause's philosophy flows from a metaphysic which, owing to its arbitrary terminology, deserves to be called enigmatic. But its most significant features are not impossible to portray.[2] Krause believes that access to philosophy is impossible for the man who does not aspire to answer the question: How can we be sure that our knowledge of things is authentic? As in the other post-Kantian idealists, the point of departure for philosophical investigation is therefore, in Krause, the formulation of a theory of knowledge. And it could be added that, as in Fichte, Schelling, or Hegel, epistemology and metaphysics are so intimately linked in Krause that they cannot be separated.

When we begin our pilgrimage toward knowledge we observe, to begin with, that the only primary knowledge which seems indisputable is that of our bodily states. These appear to us as multiple and changeable. But thanks to certain *a priori* intuitions (time, space, movement), and the functions of understanding (concepts, judgments, syllogisms), such bodily states acquire objectivity and become 'things' from which, after a fashion and up to a point, we think of ourselves as separate. So far Krause is merely accepting, with slight variations that are unimportant here, the Kantian critical method. It should be borne in mind, moreover, that in imitation of Kant, Krause does not feel obliged to explain the psychological origin of what we call 'knowing'. What interests him is simply the possibility of knowing something, and once that possibility is admitted, of proving the logical validity of knowledge. Our bodily states become matter for knowledge because, owing precisely to their multiplicity and variety, we ascribe them all to a single and stable 'something' that underlies them. This something is the *primary self*, and the vision of the primary self – *Grundschauung-Ich* – is the first link in the chain of truths that will be drawn out of that self by means of the inductive method.

Once the primary self has been revealed, Krause proceeds to induce, by analytical-subjective means, that this self is a unity in which two elements are contained: body and intellect. The self knows itself as finite for two reasons: (a) because it has to admit as indisputable the presence of other selves that limit it; and (b) because its own functions appear to it as limited. Now, the finite is what is partial, and the partial necessarily presupposes a whole which is its foundation. This whole is, according to Krause, the original or primary essence – *Urwesen* – from which arise the two elements, body and intellect, that are contained in the unity of the self. The body forms part of Nature's sphere, the intellect of Spirit's. Nature and Spirit are in their turn finite essences which, as such, postulate a higher, infinite essence, foundation of all finite essences and source of all reality. Krause calls this higher essence *Wesen*, which can be translated as Absolute Being or God. The Krausist system is, properly speaking, a *Wesenlehre* or Theory of Being.

It is easy to see that Krause uses the analytical-subjective method he has learned from Kant to correct what he considered to be a cardinal error in Kantian criticism; to wit, the conclusion that no ontological inquiry can be founded on pure reason. The existence of God, the immortality of the soul, human freedom, in short the problems with which philosophy had been concerned throughout history, were relegated by Kant to the sphere of practical reason, allowing them no other validity than that of simple postulates of moral action. Our knowledge of reality, according to Kant, is confined to phenomena. We know nothing, and can know nothing, of the 'thing-in-itself'; at most, we can *believe* in it. The theosophist in Krause refused to accept a philosophy without ontology, a philosophy he thought of as resembling a body without a head, like a system that began by throwing God out the door and ended, ashamed of so bold an action, by letting him in again through the window. It was therefore indispensable to restore ontology to the dominant position which, up to the time of Kant, very few had denied it, to restore to theoretical reason all that had been displaced to the area of practical reason, to consider the world once again as a divine creation, as a manifestation of the attributes – essentialities – of the Supreme Essence, discovered and defined by discursive understanding. In Krause's opinion it was not enough to state, for this purpose, that the only genuine knowledge is instinctive faith, the spontaneous intuition of the *noumenon*, of that which critical philosophy in particular had excluded from pure reason. A philosophy of faith or of feeling in the manner of Hamann, Herder, or Jacobi could no longer satisfy someone who knew Kant's work, and to behave as though Kant had never existed would be childish obstinacy.[3] For Krause, nothing was more repellent than Jacobi's famous phrase: 'There is light in my heart, but as soon as I try to bring it to my understanding, it vanishes.' Indeed, what seems to have led Krause to come out in partial defense of Kant was the desire to avoid the pitfalls of a philosophy based exclusively on feeling, what Hegel described as a philosophy that is the despair of all philosophy. In Hamann and especially in Jacobi Krause glimpsed the serious psychological danger that threatens every defender of a metaphysics of instinct: egotism. Eternal truth, says Krause, is not the truth that each man finds in his own heart, for the heart can easily be, and often is, mistaken. Eternal truth is that truth which the intellect discovers through methods and laws whose universal validity and acceptance cannot be doubted. If, in the immense panorama of the real, it is possible to harmonize what is disjoined, different, contradictory, that harmony is made possible only by virtue of the organizing function of reason, the quality that reason possesses of bringing order out of chaos. Krause's harmonic rationalism is, in short, an ontological reworking of Kantian criticism on the one hand, and on the other an attempt to counteract the extravagant and mystical intuitionism of the philosophers of faith.

3. Synthesis

So far we have sketched out the analytical-subjective part of Krause's metaphysics. The synthetic-objective part begins with reflection on Absolute Being. This reflection leads to the organization of a fundamental science – *Grundwissenschaft* – in which all the individual sciences are contained. It should be noted, however, that this content is purely schematic, formal; that is, it consists of a structure of principles or categories which must govern unalterably the inquiry into each of the subordinate sciences. The first four sciences deduced by Krause from fundamental science are Theory of Original Essence (*Urwesenlehre*), Science of Reason (*Vernunftwissenschaft*), Science of Nature (*Naturwissenschaft*), and Theory of Integral Essence or Anthropology (*Vereinwesenlehre*). It can now be seen that the synthetic-objective part of Krause's metaphysics follows the same path as the analytic-subjective part, but in the opposite direction. We have already seen that in the analytical part the line of inquiry ascends inductively from the basic unity of the self, through the body-intellect duality, to the higher totality of God. In the synthetic part, on the other hand, the line of inquiry begins with the higher totality of God and descends deductively, through the nature-spirit duality, to the basic unity of the self. The self is now revealed as the human individual. Man, perfect synthesis of the two finite essences of the universe, is the highest finite essence that has emerged from the hand of God.[4]

On a lower level than that of the four sciences mentioned above, the fundamental science gives rise to another group of disciplines. It must be kept in mind, in this respect, that Krause repeatedly describes his doctrine as a divine organism – *Wesengliedbau*. Every separate science or discipline is engendered in, and through, God. The concept of *organism*, whose most complete philosophical application is found in Kant, serves Krause 'as a means of dissolving multiplicity in unity without destroying multiplicity, as if in the cohesion represented by the whole, each part should acquire a higher level of existence and knowledge'.[5] Such a fusion, like that shown in the example of the living organism used by Krause to explain it, is dynamic. It is a fusion for a purpose, an intentional activity. The organic whole is simultaneously the beginning and end of each of its parts, and it can be said of each part that it fulfills its function only in the measure in which it develops whatever potential it possesses.

The separate disciplines are those that deal with the essentialities – *Wesenheiten* – of God. First among them Krause places the one he calls *Mathesis*, or science of magnitude, which studies the physico-mathematical concepts of time, space, force, movement, etc. Then comes *Logic*, the discipline that investigates the laws and forms of rational thought. *Aesthetics* occupies third place, and concerns itself with beauty as one of the attributes of the divine essence. The fourth discipline, *Ethics*, is strictly speaking the science of human life, individual as well as collective. Its object consists in determining and studying the measure in which the supreme good – also thought of as an attribute of God – is realized in the human being. Far from being a normative and regulatory discipline, based on limitations and prohibitions that are imposed on man's free activity, Krausist ethics invites man to develop fully his moral potential; and this potential is synonymous, according to Krause, with a more or less conscious aspiration to the fullness of life that springs from rational knowledge of God. The categorical imperative seems to echo through the formula 'desire and do good because it is good'. And indeed, it is in the sphere of ethics that some have seen the most conclusive proof of Krausism's relationship to the philosophy of Kant. The Krausist idea of evil was particularly fertile, and gave a humanitarian slant to the philosophy of law cultivated by so many of the philosopher's disciples. According to this idea, it is an error to attribute a positive content to evil, for by doing so one would logically reach the monstrous conclusion that, since the world is the realization in space and time of the essentialities of God, evil is one of those essentialities. Strictly speaking, for Krause, evil does not exist.[6] What is known as evil is only a partial blindness, a limitation caused by ignorance, an illusory barrier, in short, with which the man who has not yet attained a full knowledge of God and, through him, an adequate idea of the world and humanity, is obliged to struggle.

4. Panentheism

Consideration of the world of finite essences as a content of the Supreme Essence, or God, seems at first glance to give a pantheistic tinge to Krause's doctrine; and indeed Krausism's enemies, especially in Spain, frequently pointed out the immanentist nature of the system. The fact that Krause's terminology is obscure and equivocal has meant that his thought has sometimes lent itself, even in some of his disciples, to confusions that are not entirely unjustified. Even Amiel himself considers it obvious that Krausist philosophy is a philosophy of immanence.[7] And yet it would be well to remember, in this respect, that Krause turned his back on his teacher Schelling precisely because the latter was a pantheist, and that he coined a new word, *panentheism*, or doctrine of *everything in God*, in an attempt to go beyond what he considered to be limitations, rather than errors, in the doctrines of immanence and transcendence.[8]

The relationship between God and the world to which panentheism aspires is a perfect illustration of Krause's dialectical method. The doctrine of *everything in God* is the synthesis in which the historical opposition between pantheism and deism is resolved and transcended. In Krause's opinion, it is necessary to protect the basic truth that underlies both doctrines; namely, the inclination on the one hand to make the world divine, and on the other the assertion of the independence of man's ethical acts. Krause criticized the pantheistic view of the world proposed by Schelling because it leads inevitably to the view of history as a simple natural process, a sort of 'divine determinism' in which there would be no room for the ideas of human freedom and responsibility. To overcome this obstacle, panentheism has recourse to the following formula: 'The world is not outside God...nor is it God himself, but it is in God and through God.'[9] This seems to mean (a) that the world does not exhaust, nor even contain, God's total essence; (b) that the world occupies, in relation to God, a subordinate but not independent place, or, stated in other terms, that God freely thinks, feels, and wills the world, that God posits the world as a moment of the divine essence;

(c) that what we call world is the totality of manifestations of the divine essence in time and space; and (d) that knowledge of the world is knowledge of the divine essence and its manifestations. It should be pointed out that Krause, in determining the link between God and the world, is obliged to distinguish two forms of causality in God: eternal causality (*God-principle*), which recognizes the world's immanence in God, and temporal causality (*God-cause*) according to which God is the transcendent, supreme, and free creator of the universe. The consideration of what is called 'life' as a 'moment in God' is, in the eyes of Krause's disciples, the chief merit of panentheism.

5. Philosophy of history

Because the *Philosophy of history* is the last and most important of the disciplines that Krause deduces from fundamental science by the synthetic-objective method, it merits fairly leisurely treatment even in this rapid overview of the Krausist system. Like any other particular science or discipline, the philosophy of history arises from Krause's religious conception of the world. What we call *world* is, as has been stated above, a freely determined moment in God. Hence the eternal exists in, and is revealed through, the temporal, and the task of the historian or philosopher of history consists in discovering, underneath the multiple forms of historical event, the self-determinations of the divine essence. According to Krause, every genuinely historiographical task involves a philosophical labor. The historian who limited himself to more or less impartially describing mere historical *event* would display a distorted idea of his mission, for the particular, the *positive* element in history is intelligible only as a limited and partial manifestation of the divine essence. In Krause's philosophy a distinction is made between internal and external history – 'true' and 'quasi-true' history respectively – a distinction which, in the course of time, was destined to find favor among historians and philosophers and merits particular attention in our day, when an exaggerated form of historicism is so much in vogue. Internal, that is, authentic history, is always a formal history – or, if you like, a history of ideas. 'Ideas', writes Krause, 'are the torch which must light up the eyes and path of the historical researcher who seeks reality.'[10] The contradiction between ideas and the chaos of historical events is only an apparent one. As opposed to the criterion of the extreme rationalist, for whom the reason-history contrast is equivalent to the *form-deformation* opposition, Krause prefers the *idea-ideal* pairing, in which the second element is not the antithesis but only the partial actualization of the first. *Idea* is always the *idea of God*; *ideal* is the *ideal of humanity*, humanity's constant aspiration to the fullness of its terrestrial existence.[11] And it must be emphasized that fullness of life is possible only when knowledge of the divine essence and its temporal manifestations is achieved. The exclusive aim of a genuine philosophy of history is to study the *idea of God* in successive stages of humanity's evolution, without losing sight of the fact that such an *idea* within time is, when examined from a different point of view, a chronicle of the development of man's intellectual and moral faculties.

If we are to understand the essential traits of Krause's philosophy of history, we must examine once again the dialectical nature of the metaphysic from which it proceeds. In its analytical as well as its synthetic aspect, knowledge starts off from a simple unity, passes through a stage of differentiation, and ends with the harmonization of opposites in a higher unity. These three periods of dialectical movement correspond to the three ages that can be discerned in the existence of all finite creatures: infancy, youth, and maturity, or, if you will, indifferentiation, opposition, and harmony.[12] This is – and it cannot be too strongly emphasized – a general law, inexorably reigning in every time and place. From the unity of God, which simultaneously contains in itself and transcends all finite essences and all possible oppositions, there is a descent through opposition to the finite unity which is man. Man's gradual return to unity with God, supreme aspiration of the human individual, is the true content of history. The adequate interpretation of that return demands that the philosopher-historian establish, over and above the confusion of historical events, the three stages into which the process of man's reintegration with his Maker is divided. These three stages are, as can be deduced, those of indifferentiation, opposition, and harmony, and correspond respectively to humanity's infancy, youth, and maturity. In each of them the idea that man has formed about God offers a particular aspect. Actually they are three conceptions of the world, three perspectives through which the human individual has successively looked upon his Creator, on himself, and on his fellow human beings.[13]

The first stage therefore corresponds to the infancy of human societies. Primitive man is a rudimentary being placed in a world where the individual factor does not yet exist. His life is spent in blissful unconsciousness: he exists submerged in a whole which is neither explained nor explainable. His notion of God is simple and immediate, something like the idea a nursing child has of its mother: complete dependence and unlimited confidence – in a word, indifferentiation. Primitive man's view of things is insufficient, because it is confused, to allow him to affirm his initiative and freedom of action in and through those things. On the other hand, his embryonic mentality makes him incapable of particularization. With God, as with the world and himself, he lives in a fundamental unity which Krause believes to be the initial phase of history. It is a simple and innocent existence which later periods, who had received it only as a faraway echo, would poeticize in the myth of the earthly paradise.

The second stage, that of opposition, corresponds to humanity's youth. Little by little man begins to recognize the things that he finds around him; he learns to distinguish one from another and is attracted by them in his turn. Human activity, which is above all a desire for possession, a means of exercising the urge for domination – in short, a declaration of independence – is lavished on the physical milieu. Man observes his increasing energy and skill, and slowly turns away from that simple and fundamental unity in which he had lived with God in earliest times. But even after the separation between man and God has taken place, it cannot be said that man's religious impulse has weakened, merely that it has assumed a different aspect as a result of man's new-found preoccupation with the world of sensorial experience. What in the previous age had been blind instinct, unconscious submission, now becomes food for the imagination. After he has lost God, man feels compelled to rediscover him, seeking him in the inanimate or animate things that he sees on every hand. The fetichist's crude religion, the cult of natural forces, of heroes, of man-gods, even the beautiful and delicate polytheism of the Greeks, are only manifestations of the desire to find God in the world of the senses.[14] The common factor in all these religions is that they are materializations of the imagination. In this second phase of history moral qualities are just beginning to appear. And it is interesting to note that precisely in the cases where they display exceptional development – as proof, we may recall the Greek philosophers and Roman moralists – polytheism is emptied of religious content and sinks to the level of pure convention or poetic myth. Nor is this surprising, for man's moral faculties absolutely demand the unity of God as the source and cause of all reality.

The third stage, of which our present historical period forms part, begins when man turns his attention to himself and discovers in the depths of his consciousness the image of the one God, creator and ruler of life. But it must be noted that this is not a primary discovery. What man primarily discovers is the unity of his own consciousness. Underneath the multiplicity and variety of his psychic and physical states, he realizes that something exists which underlies them and links them all together, something that is both unique and constant, the origin and purpose of the infinite modalities into which his existence is condensed. If previously he has lived in the dimension of imagination, which required an external and centrifugal kind of activity, now he lives more and more in the area of understanding, of internal activity, which attracts and orders the chaotic impressions that pour in upon him at every instant. In the end he knows that he is one and the same, because he feels capable of interpreting the fundamental cohesion that underlies the chaos of his life. This conviction of his own capacity leads him to a new evaluation of his power, his worth, his mission. What is commonly called 'human dignity' is the realization that man achieves of his essential integrity. But this discovery does not satisfy him completely. He does not live in isolation in the world, nor are his faculties (though considerable) limitless. He observes that he is surrounded by innumerable life forms. Around him crowd a vast number of men like himself, on whom he instinctively confers attributes identical to those he recognizes in himself. And, by reflecting on his own unity and contrasting it with the variety of all the rest, he begins to grasp the idea of a higher Consciousness, one and the same as well, infinite in time and space, which serves as support and link for all finite beings. In short, the discovery of the unity of his own consciousness brings man to the discovery of God's oneness.

Monotheism, therefore, marks the prelude to man's maturity. It is the turning point which, by correcting what has been up to that time a gradual withdrawal from God, places the human being in a process of return to him. Knowledge of the One God 'immediately causes a renascence in the whole man, arouses a new life-voice in the concert of reason, understanding, and imagination'.[15] Henceforth the process of his spiritual perfection will take the form of a slow refinement of the idea of God, whose attributes, freed from the anthropomorphism of the previous stage, will assume their true significance, channel human activity, and assist in the realization of the noble ends to which man can and must aspire. But observe that, according to Krause, this task of purification is both slow and arduous. After all, history is only the projection in time of man's innumerable hesitations and false starts in his tireless journey toward God. The annals of monotheism offer abundant proofs that, even after having grasped the unity of God, man still falls short of the fullness of life which knowledge of that unity ought to involve. The Jewish nation is monotheistic, but its monotheism is narrow and nationalistic, a simple opposition of the One God to the plural God of the Gentiles. Yet Jewish monotheism's lack of perfection does not derive solely from the deep-rooted sense of uniqueness that has been injected into it, but because in addition the Hebrew idea of divine unity does not arise from rational apprehension but is received by tradition. This is due to the fact that the Jewish people did not come to monotheism during their mature phase, 'but received that idea during their early period...establishing themselves in it without cultivating and applying it freely, and hence, except for a few superior men, most of the [Jewish] people viewed God as nothing more than a powerful national lord'.[16]

From Judaic monotheism to that established by Jesus, considerable progress was made. Christianity proclaimed love among men and the submission of all humanity to a common Father. However, Christian doctrine cannot escape the law of history, and this demands that every stage in man's spiritual maturation involve surpassing the previous stages. History does not tolerate the great leap. It is possible that at a given moment an individual could arise whose stunning intuition was appropriate to a spiritual level much higher than the one reigning during his lifetime. In the long run, however, the realization of that intuitive vision would be subject to the inescapable principle of historical evolution. Jesus' doctrine is one of those intuitions that rend the veil of the future. 'My kingdom is not of this time', could have been the Nazarene's sorrowful conclusion. It is not strange, therefore, that the chronicle of Christianity shows us the incapacity of many Christians to understand and properly apply the Master's teachings:

From the beginning, [Christian doctrine] was adulterated in many ways by residues of both Judaic and Gentile doctrines; it was applied only to relationships in individual life, and social entities were left outside it or were unsatisfactorily linked to its spirit. Slavery and tyranny continued to reign for a long time in Christian society...Denial and mortification of the body, an ungrateful attitude toward Nature, its beauty and its laws, persecution of dissidents, heresies, inquisition, mass assassinations of youthful nations...civil and religious wars, internal disunity and demoralization of the better nations, such have been the effects of imperfect knowledge of God's unity and the love of men in God, as taught by Jesus Christ.[17]

As a religious doctrine Christianity is irreproachable. It is men who have been unable to raise themselves to the moral level implicit in the Christian concept of the world.

For that level, let us repeat, will be attainable only when man, sweeping away the darkness in which he has lived and still lives, acquires consummate knowledge of God, of himself, and of his fellow man. It must also be remembered that according to Krause such a period of plenitude was not far off, or better still was already faintly visible on the horizon. Man, the prodigal son, was on the point of returning to his Father's house. He had left it when still a child, impelled by curiosity about the world of the senses. Nature had been his first, adolescent love, and he had paid her homage under the various forms of polytheism. Later a spiritual type of monotheism had displaced the naturalistic, plural paganism, and it – during the somber and penitent reaction of Christianity's first centuries – had led man to spurn the world of the senses and accept, along with the suffocating influence of a priestly class, a theocratic and static interpretation of society. Only with the awakening of the scientific spirit had man come to understand that he is a combination of nature and spirit, and that the full life requires the harmony of these two essential elements. The truly blessed time will be that in which men live closely bound together by mutual love and knowledge, when they work in cooperation to achieve the total development of the spiritual energies latent in them, and in which they recognize God as the first and final cause of life.

All men and all humanity will be raised into God, they will live more faithful to their eternal destiny, more in harmony with the life of the world in higher spheres, those of nature as well as the spirit. All men will know each other and love one another like a family of children of God, and destined to be reunited in the fullness of the divine life, and in that ultimate hope they will rebuild their history as a new construction.[18]

3

Catechumens and nonconformists

1. In praise of eccentricity

In the spiritual history of any country there are periods when certain sensitive persons discover in themselves a silent irritation with respect to reigning ideas and beliefs. It might be said that their day-to-day surroundings depress them, that their vital horizons seem to contract; and when they experience the stifling sensation that ensues, they tend to withdraw into themselves and seek shelter in the depths of their own consciousness against a world that has become intolerable to them, they are not quite sure why. Such periods of introversion are eminently periods of definition and analysis. Generally speaking, they are also periods of unusual intellectual honesty. At such moments, cultivating one's own garden is a praiseworthy task; but before doing so, it would not be a bad idea to begin by setting limits, by building a barrier between one's private territory and that of others. Once this spiritual property has been enclosed, however, it becomes obvious that it contains a mixture of real and imaginary assets, and consequently there must be a further process of delimitation between them. The ensuing operation consists in setting aside the ideas and beliefs that are considered suspect; that is, all those which have infiltrated one's mind through indolence or inattention without having been subjected to previous scrutiny. A halt must be cried and the password demanded not only of that which is clearly fraudulent, but also of everything received from tradition, everything outworn or purely routine. The final and at the same time most painful task is that of uprooting everything that has turned out to be unacceptable in this work of purification.

Perhaps not much will be left after the conclusion of such an examination of conscience, but the residue, the irreducible nucleus of individual personality, will be of enormous value. However, if the individual contents himself, like the miser counting his gold, with making an inventory of all that is truly his, his task will have been barren. But the fact is that in such periods the withdrawal of an intelligent and sensitive man is merely temporary. Really it is a question of true *askesis*, a sort of training period that will allow him to return to the fray with energies equal to the magnitude of the struggle in which he expects to participate.

A dual responsibility weighs on such men. On the one hand they must strip their thoughts bare under the inquisitorial eye of their own conscience, must take on humility and jettison prejudice; they must bring arguments to bear and, when these are insufficient, they must harbor fruitful doubts, without forgetting that the inner balance to which they aspire will be precarious at best, a medley of certainties and anxieties. Like those other practitioners of asceticism, the anchorites in the wilderness, these also are assailed by numberless temptations. The most seductive and dangerous of these is the tendency to revel in their withdrawal from the world, to think of mundane affairs as unworthy of any man whose sights are set high. The ivory tower, like the monk's cell, often leads a man to the Buddhistic enjoyment of his own excellence. The recluse shut in his ivory tower who distills his wisdom drop by drop runs the risk of falling prey to selfishness and arrogance. But we need not concern ourselves with these high priests of misanthropy. Those who do not aspire to perpetual isolation willingly take upon themselves – and this is their other obligation – the task of confronting the indifference, mockery, or ill-will of their contemporaries. They neither can nor should seek to be understood, for their mission consists in sowing unrest and anxieties, in whipping up sluggish spirits and censuring faint-hearted attitudes. Cynics will attack them, attributing to their words and deeds the only motive universally recognized by ordinary mortals: self-interest. They will be labeled egotists or charlatans, or at the very least eccentrics. Only a small company of men with similar viewpoints will come to share their labors, and these will be simultaneously disciples, interpreters, and popularizers; and the acceptance given to the master's teachings will depend in large part on their fidelity and enthusiasm. But it must be remembered that, first of all, much of the essence of a doctrine or a teaching evaporates during the course of its transference, and that the rest is attenuated and diluted as it gradually expands among an ever larger number of catachumens.

2. Personality cult or ideocracy?

The preceding considerations may help us to explain the singular case of Julián Sanz del Río, for in fact we are dealing with a phenomenon unprecedented in the history of Spanish thought. Neither his intellectual gifts, which though genuine were certainly not extraordinary, nor his doctrine, which was as difficult to grasp in its Spanish form as in the German original, give grounds for the influence exercised for so many years by this professor at the University of Madrid. With a few minor exceptions, the impression given by his writings is that of a rather limited thinker, dedicated to the task of building a philosophical edifice which, owing to its enormous proportions and abstruse materials, was fated never to rise higher than its foundations. Among the numerous anomalies displayed by the Spanish Krausist movement – and strictly speaking all of it was a huge anomaly – the most surprising is the fact that only a very small number of Sanz del Río's disciples ever really penetrated into the master's thought. And into Krause's, it need hardly be said, fewer still. For example, it is revealing that when Manuel de la Revilla was asked by the *Revista Contemporánea* to review Sanz del Río's most important book, *Análisis del pensamiento racional*, published posthumously in 1877, he should have performed the task with this remarkable comment: 'We cannot offer a judgment because, thanks to the very special language used by Señor Sanz del Río, it is impossible to understand the doctrines contained in this book.'[1] And his words are all the more surprising because it is well known that Revilla had been an assiduous visitor to the classroom at the University of Madrid where Sanz del Río had orally propounded those same doctrines. If we now turn to the Krausist leader's non-professional writings in search of enlightenment, we will also be disappointed. His letters, at least those so far published, are notable for their lack of intimacy, of human warmth, and must be thought of chiefly as sketches of work projects, glosses on his professional labors, and commentaries on the schools representing post-Kantian idealism. These letters, seven in all, were published by Manuel de la Revilla in the *Revista Europea* between 15 March and 26 April 1874, and were preceded by a note in which Revilla assured his readers that:

through them...will be gained, better perhaps than from the rest of his works, knowledge of the man as well as the philosopher, and it will be understood how much abnegation, sublimity, and true greatness there was in that life, as exemplary as it was fruitful, misunderstood by the ignorant and frivolous, held up to ridicule by those who are incapable of sensing greatness or accomplishing anything good, and unworthily vilified by the enemies of science and civilization.[2]

Now, what is not sensed at all in those letters is precisely the 'knowledge of the man' to which Revilla refers. The man slips away from us among the dense foliage of philosophical speculation and the studied objectivity of a language burdened with technical terms. And yet the fact is that it was this man, the particular man named Sanz del Río, who captivated with his overpowering personality a group of men who were themselves vigorous personalities. His disciples and friends are unable to transmit to us the nature of this magnetic attraction. The praises they shower on him, mostly after his death, are insipidly conventional and reveal that stage in human relationships when a luminous presence has congealed into remembrance, and affection into veneration. Nor do his adversaries come nearer the mark, in spite of the fact that it is usually easier to define what repels one about a person than what attracts. The most energetic of his enemies, Menéndez Pelayo, limited himself to remarking that Sanz del Río 'possessed a special and diabolical art' for fascinating youth.[3]

Captivate, fascinate, seduce: these are perhaps the words that best describe the activities of the leader of the Spanish Krausist movement. And note that by 'activities' is understood here not his strictly teaching activity, but that which overflowed the confines of the classroom and spilled out into the private life of both master and disciples. In the concrete case with which we are dealing here, it was not in the chair at the University of Madrid but in the modest flat on the Calle de San Vicente that the master gleaned his most important triumphs. In that atmosphere of homely intimacy the cold impersonality of his platform oratory broke down into cordial dialogue, took on the impassioned tone of friendly argument or the calm one of a family chat, and each listener in turn felt that he was being singled out from the others, momentarily raised to the master's level. In the symphony of conversation each recognized passages from his favorite melody. The doubt and hope, the discouragement and rebelliousness, the unfocused fervor and rude sincerity of the young and untried soul, all passed in review before that Socratic symposium under the spell of a man for whom there was, as he himself admitted, 'no finer mission...than that of attracting, persuading, and instructing those in whom the idea of humanity, daughter of God, freedom, and tolerance still lie sleeping'.[4] And what so deeply astonished Menéndez Pelayo, Laverde, Orti y Lara, Navarro Villoslada, Alonso Martínez, and other prominent antagonists of the Krausist leader was that a considerable portion of Spanish youth was ready to be fascinated by Sanz del Río's 'honeyed words', perhaps for the simple reason that in those days there were very few professors who took a genuine interest in youth. More than anything else, the chair provided a means of enhancing its holder's personal prestige, a prestige indispensable to anyone interested in courting the much more exciting favors offered by politics or literature. But a professor completely wrapped up in his teaching labors and possessed, in addition, with a desire to shake up lazy minds was something extremely unusual at the time in Spanish university circles. Under such circumstances the response of youth could hardly be anything but fervent. Rather than to Krausist doctrine, tribute was offered to the man who professed it, to the individual named Julián Sanz del Río. 'Austere, perceptive, always generous and cordial...tolerant and respectful of all ideas...he accepted life as a very lofty duty', his biographer Gervasio Manrique writes of him; '...the teacher whose memory I revere', declares Francisco de Paula Canalejas; Manuel de la Revilla calls him 'a distinguished man'. The Spaniard's well-known fondness for the whole man, any one of whose activities, no matter how significant, is always less important than the man himself, is apparent in the enthusiasm for Sanz del Río displayed not only by his disciples but also by many others who never came to know him personally. Those who received his teaching and guidance, even those who in the course of time deserted the ranks of Krausism, evoke first of all the friend in whose delightful company their love for studies in philosophy, law, literature, and history had sprung to life.

We must emphasize the nature of this relationship – more personal than doctrinal – because sometimes it appeared under aspects that lent themselves to facile caricature. There was a time, for instance, when Sanz del Río's disciples and admirers adopted rather strange ways of behaving in public, about which there is no lack of comment in newspaper articles of the period. The Krausists dressed soberly, usually in black; their faces were fixed in an impassive and severe expression, they walked with a preoccupied air, cultivated taciturnity, and when they spoke did so in a quiet, slow voice, sprinkling their sentences with axioms that were often intentionally obscure, avoided frivolous amusements, and seldom frequented cafés and theaters. Needless to say, nothing in Krausist precepts justified this line of conduct. But its explanation is not far to seek. The Krausists, no doubt out of a rather ingenuous and puerile admiration, imitated the appearance, clothing, gestures, and preferences of Sanz del Río himself. For them, the Krausist word had been made flesh in their much-admired teacher, to the point that eventually it became impossible for them to distinguish the doctrinal part of him from the personal part. Many supposed Krausists went no further, indeed, than to copy the head of the school in external appearance.

But what began as trivial imitation ended by assuming characteristics of conscious differentiation. Gradually the young Krausists realized that Sanz del Río's particular traits, his peculiarities, represented the antithesis of everything that was conventional and conformist in the period's social life, and that, in consequence, when they took over those peculiarities they were indirectly rejecting what the majority practiced. Like any small nucleus with reformist ambitions, as time went on the Krausist group expressed ever more insistently its attitude of protest against existing conditions, perhaps simply because those conditions had ceased to exist, if the paradox be permitted; they persisted only in the hollow veneration of a vulgar 'presbytocracy', as Unamuno was later to say. It is not strange, therefore, that even in details as unimportant as the way of dressing or the timbre of their voices, the catechumens of the Krausist group tried to find a way to distinguish themselves from *the others*, to raise a barrier not so much to protect themselves as better to combat routine, vulgarity, and hypocrisy. In the last years of Isabella II's reign, which Gómez de Baquero describes as absurdly optimistic, the leaders of the Krausist movement made a tacit appeal to seriousness. For them, taking life seriously meant taking in sail, withdrawing within themselves, searching in the secret places of their consciousness for an explanation of the universal mystery. For the general tendency of that period consisted in exactly the opposite. One lived from day to day, getting the most one could out of each moment, frivolously squandering energies of which a deteriorating country stood in critical need. And the most urgent task was to contain this wastage, to stanch the hemorrhage that threatened to destroy the nation's very existence. Hence the Krausists' insistence on living according to a pattern of austerity, moderation, and circumspection. No one has described this noble desire to take life seriously better than Galdós. León Roch, the prototype of the young Krausist, does his best to adjust his life to an ideal based on full utilization of his own spiritual resources. 'He had', his creator says of him, 'magnificent plans, among them the plan of giving his own thought the mission of informing life, making himself the

absolute master of life and making it bow to the tyranny of the idea.'
It was an ambitious desire, irrevocably destined to failure because, as
Galdós adds:

> the men who dream of this grandiose victory do not take into account the
> power of what we might call *social destiny*, an enormous and enslaving
> power, composed of beliefs held by ourselves and others, of invincible
> obstinacies both collective and individual, of errors and of virtue itself, of
> a thousand things which simultaneously demand both scorn and respect
> and, finally, of the laws and customs with whose arrogant stability it is
> neither licit nor possible, usually, to engage in pitched battle.[5]

It is the tragedy of the man who wants to live in conformity with the
principles of reason. León Roch professes ideas that are in patent
disagreement with the atmosphere of fraud, hypocrisy, and fanaticism
in which he lives. Far from weakening in the face of general hostility,
he analyzes his thoughts, and this analysis confirms him more and more
in his convictions. His ideas become rigid, acquire cutting edges that
deal out wounds to right and left. Constantly besieged by aggressive
ignorance and burning fanaticism, he gradually loses his serenity and
moderation of spirit. And, a sectarian of the opposite persuasion from
the sectarianism all around him, he ends by betraying, greatly to his
sorrow, the noble standard with which he had hoped to rule his life.

3. The nature of Krausist proselytism

Among many others, one of the most serious accusations made against
Sanz del Río was the imputation that in his work he was led by a desire
to surround himself with a group of wholly loyal followers who, having
been strictly indoctrinated in the new philosophy and blinded to any
other influence, would rush to overthrow the values of traditional Spain
and pervert unsuspecting youth. According to its detractors, Krausism
had to prepare the ground by infiltrating centers of middle and higher
education, especially the University of Madrid, which, since it was the
most prestigious as well as the place where the school's leader did his
teaching, was the one most likely to serve as a center of dispersal for the
new doctrines. Sanz del Río's enemies did not hesitate to insist repeatedly that he rewarded his adepts' loyalty by distributing professor-
ships in secondary schools and universities among them, like so many
Islands of Barataria.[6]

This accusation was a natural conclusion of the thesis upheld by
those who supported traditional and ultramontane ideas; according to

this thesis, Krausism was a sort of secret society dedicated body and soul to the sinister aim of destroying Spain's religious unity and subverting her political and social structure. That is why attention was drawn, sometimes surreptitiously and sometimes openly, to supposed resemblances between the Krausist school and freemasonry. Menéndez Pelayo maintained that the group around Sanz del Río was a Masonic lodge in disguise. The well-known fact that Krause had played an important role in German freemasonry gave no little support to the insinuation of Masonic affiliation. But on the other hand it was also a fact that Krause, at last becoming annoyed by the society's secrecy and puerile rites, had eventually broken all ties with it.[7]

However, without excluding the possibility that one Krausist or another may have rendered homage to the Great Architect of the Universe in some secret lodge, it is wholly ridiculous to suggest that Sanz del Río and his disciples had any intention of engaging in activity of a secret nature. Krausist philosophy was taught openly in the University of Madrid and the public platform of the Madrid Athenaeum. The small circle in the Calle de San Vicente required no initiation ceremony except an interest in subjects a little more exalted than those that were discussed around the table of any café, and the patience necessary to decipher a nomenclature which was at first sight incomprehensible. As if this were not enough, the new doctrine's messianic nature, its propaedeutic function with regard to a better future life, the need to make some impression on people's attention if it wished to carry out the task it had set for itself, all forced it inexorably toward public activity. To withdraw into itself would have meant not only courting atrophy but distorting the original purpose, that of a redemptive mission, set forth by the school's founder Krause. This purpose had been fully corroborated by the German philosopher's most prominent disciples: Leonhardi, Ahrens, Röder, Tiberghien. And as early as 1844, when he was still a student in Heidelberg, Sanz del Río himself had indicated the line of conduct he intended to follow on his return to Spain: 'Precisely', he wrote to José de la Revilla, 'one of the perfections of Krause's doctrine is that it can accommodate itself perfectly to the human spirit's different levels of culture; and even today I am considering...what part [of it] I will teach, and how I will teach it, in my own country, so that the life of the spirit and the love of truth will quicken among us naturally and gradually.'[8]

To quicken spiritual life and the love of truth: but it is worth asking, truth seen from the vantage point of Krausist philosophy? Was Sanz del Río really the narrow and fanatical spirit his enemies have described to us? Did he carry his teaching to the extreme of rejecting any interpretation of truth other than that supported by Krause's philosophy? If we are to answer these questions satisfactorily we must begin by distinguishing between the two aspects – the speculative and the instructional – into which the Krausist leader's intellectual personality was split. That Sanz del Río himself had recognized very early the dual direction his activity was taking is proved by a perusal of the first letter he wrote to José de la Revilla in 1844. In it the apprentice philosopher took special care to separate those elements in his intellectual formation exclusively incumbent on himself from those which had to do with the teaching commission he had received from the Spanish government. About his profound personal advocacy of Krausist doctrine he left no doubt whatever: 'My inner and complete conviction regarding the truth of Krause's doctrine...does not spring from purely external motives...but is produced directly and immediately by the very doctrine that I find within myself.'[9] That is, he openly claimed the right to think in accordance with the demands of his spirit. But he added, in justification of his preference:

I chose that [system] which, according to the little I was able to understand of it, I found most consistent, most complete, most in agreement with the dictates of good judgment on the points where that judgment can operate, and, especially, [the system] most susceptible to a practical application... these and no others had to be the characteristics of the doctrine that would satisfy my country's intellectual needs.

Elsewhere he proclaimed that 'my unchanging resolution is to consecrate all my strength, throughout my life, to the study, explanation, and propagation of this doctrine, insofar as it is adaptable and useful to our country'. From this it can be inferred that even then Sanz del Río understood the necessity, or at least the desirability, of setting limits to his future teaching labors. Dissemination of the new doctrine ought to respond first of all to the country's intellectual needs, to carry out fully a practical and useful purpose. But 'usefulness', if we are not mistaken, was understood here in a dual sense. On the one hand it was necessary to reactivate the inclination for work and mental discipline and a general interest in science among the youth of Spain, as a first step toward modernization of university studies. On the other, it was essential to persuade both reactionaries and doubters that Krausist doctrine, despite its exotic origin, contained nothing that could be repugnant to the Spanish genius, the forms of Spanish culture, or the spiritual aspirations of the race. On the contrary, it would afford the educated Spaniard the means of obtaining a complete as well as dispassionate knowledge of himself and his possibilities.

In the long run, however, it was unlikely that Sanz del Río, adhering with so much faith to the new doctrine, could be satisfied with placing it at the service of a utilitarian purpose, no matter how urgent or highminded that purpose might be. Krausism, to be sure, offered an exhortatory aspect to talented and sensitive persons; it prescribed rules of conduct, outlined ideals worthy of humanity's high destiny. But underneath this practical structure, sustaining it as the notion of right sustains the law, rested abstract metaphysical principles to which a merely receptive attitude and a lively intelligence did not provide adequate access. And, in addition, it was necessary to undergo rigid training from which any deviation toward the purely utilitarian was specifically excluded. Hence it is not at all strange that in 1862, once the introductory and popularizing phase of his task had ended – insofar as he was concerned – with the publication of his *Ideal de la Humanidad*, Sanz del Río should have written to his disciple Francisco de Paula Canalejas: 'This conviction [of the absolute superiority of Krause's system] arouses another strong wish and inner desire in me...that of imparting it to a few spirits well equipped for the task, ready to do it and free from more pressing interests or occupations, or from completely preconceived and inflexible ideas which have run their intellectual course.'[10] Did he have any illusions about the viability of his project? He candidly admitted that he did not. He complained, first of all, about 'the rarity of such spirits nowadays, owing to the difficulty of a person's being so clear and free and consistent with himself'; he also recognized personal deficiencies that would hinder his purpose: '...although certain and clear in my conviction,' he said, 'I am still unskilled in demonstrating it to another person, in conformity with his individual rationality'; and lastly, he indicated that his physical complaints prevented him from undertaking a task which, in order to be effective, would require all his strength.[11] Hence the project was never more than a beautiful illusion. Sanz del Río had indeed cherished the idea of forming a school, of surrounding himself with a group of young enthusiasts, each of whom, 'in conformity with his individual rationality', would have received instruction and help from the master. But note how different this proposed school was from the one which, according to the Krausist movement's detractors, operated effectively and secretly in Spanish teaching circles. If the project had a flaw, it was that of excessive ingenuousness, for the philosophical society of anchorites envisioned by Sanz del Río merits no other assessment. Those who were to share with him the task of working out Krause's doctrine in detail would have had to sever, as an indispensable pre-requisite, all the ties linking them to the world of material interests and concerns, a separation extremely difficult at any time and practically impossible in the Spain of Isabella II. Even to cultivate 'the interior realm', it is doubtful that the most enthusiastic of Krausists would have aspired to imitate the master in his retreat at Illescas. Most of his disciples intended, as was natural, to lead an active life. For them Krausism served as a new ideological tool whose effectiveness, of which they were theoretically convinced, was in urgent need of demonstration in the various spheres of practical life.

4. Krausism's elect

At first sight, it is hard to reconcile the desire for withdrawal displayed by Sanz del Río in 1862 with the proselytizing campaign into which Krause's doctrine forced him by its very nature. But the really para-doxical thing was that he felt terrified by the unexpected success his teachings had achieved. In the less than five years between his *Discurso* at the University of Madrid in October, 1857, and the letter to Canalejas in June, 1862, Krausism had made considerable progress in intellectual circles. There were already numerous adepts among univer-sity and secondary-school teachers, and young men who had been initiated into the 'brand-new philosophy' were beginning to emerge from the classrooms eager to propagate it in their turn. In the Madrid Athenaeum the Krausists held sway with little opposition. And to cap the climax Don Fernando de Castro, Queen Isabella's honorary chaplain, had preached a sermon in the sovereign's presence in Novem-ber, 1861, in which he interpreted the evolution of religious ideas from an openly Krausist viewpoint. The notoriety aroused by this sermon marked the beginning of the bitter religious disputes to which the new doctrine gave rise in the years immediately preceding the Revolution of 1868.[12]

However, Sanz del Río thought he saw in this apparently flattering result a serious danger to the purity and integrity of the philosophy he professed. He correctly surmised that, with very few exceptions, those who flocked to the Krausist ranks were seeking not metaphysical principles or methods of reasoning, but whatever the doctrine offered of more or less definite conclusions, of propositions serviceable for an immediate program of political, social, or religious reforms. He observed with disenchantment that there were others who 'Krausistified', as the word of the day had it, simply to be in fashion, putting on the most superficial aspects of the doctrine as if it were a showy costume and reducing it to a handful of frivolous slogans. If this was going to be the final result of his efforts, the new philosophy would have a hard struggle to survive in its authentic essentiality, in its claim to be rigorous metaphysical speculation, far above any immediate practical application or as a source of fleeting ideological enthusiasms. The certainty expressed from time to time by Sanz del Río that Krause's system represented a triumph over all the imperfections and contradictions of history was, as he himself recognized, the result of a spiritual preference which predisposed him, in advance of all reasoning, to believe that the Krausist view of the world was the true one. But his penetration, out of sheer sympathy as it were, of Krause's thought was not enough. It had to be sustained upon a rational foundation, to be justified without fear of failure to his own conscience, as a prior requisite to any attempt at effective propagation. *The fervor of the imagination* had to become *rational certainty*. And indeed all of Sanz del Río's activities, after his return to Spain in 1844, revolved around the problem of how to accomplish this change. To the insistence of his friends, who constantly urged him to publish some sample or preliminary sketch of his long task, he replied that everything would be achieved with patience: 'Leave me in peace with myself', he wrote to Canalejas in May, 1862, '...for between my natural desire to speak my thoughts in the public forum and the insistence – so important for me – of my friends, I might be led into the temptation of doing something precipitately, and outside its proper time.' And he added somewhat testily, 'Superficial idealism immediately absorbs any idea that makes an impression on it, and does not rest until it has brought that idea to light. But philosophical reason has higher and more serious duties, if it is to defend its rightful place today, its claim to primacy and superiority in the face of historical *public reason*.'[13]

And so Sanz del Río had reached a crossroads, and had resolutely taken the less attractive of the two roads that lay before him. The most tempting and perhaps the most comfortable path would have been that of public activity. The moment could not have been more propitious. Traditional institutions, which for some time had shown yawning cracks, were threatening imminent collapse. The absence up to that time of a genuinely intellectual and critical class, capable of disseminating new ideas and demolishing old ones, had been the cause of the deplorable superficiality of Spanish life. There was constant talk of innovating, of correcting, but any attempted change was merely a slight alteration of the epidermis, one more wrinkle on the country's ageing face. People lacked direction, and under such circumstances it is conceivable that they might have rushed to follow anyone who, eschewing the rhetorical phrase and the theatrical gesture, would offer to serve as a guide. The fact that Sanz del Río turned his back on the possibility of entering public life was the result of his natural timidity on the one hand and on the other his unalterable belief that it was useless to hasten events. According to the philosophy of history he had learned in Krause, the future triumph of his doctrine was inevitable. It mattered little whether that triumph came soon or late. The Krausist vision of the world, like fruit on a tree, would ripen at its proper season, and neither impatience nor personal whim could hasten or delay the inexorable process. He reminded those who thought that the time had come for direct intervention in the affairs of the day that their impetuosity was distorting the historical law on which the new philosophy was based. Vehemence is a trait of the man who is unsure of himself. The cool, serene man is the one who knows how to wait, who has learned the secret of waiting till the appropriate moment. 'The thought that guides me', said Sanz del Río, '[shows] with irresistible truth...that it is real time which fashions and brings forth the thing.'[14] There was no need to trust appearances that might well be deceptive. Now more than ever, when acceptance of the more accessible portion of Krausist philosophy seemed assured, a strict watch must be kept so that the essential part of the doctrine, that is, the method of scientific investigation, would not be weakened in the rush to find solutions for the immediate problems of practical life. Because of this need, his most faithful friends must be ready to follow the master along a path opposite to that of public applause. The thinker-teacher insisted:

This doctrine must exist for a long time yet in latent form and putting down roots, and even though it *filters through* to the public...it must not and cannot speak directly in public, and still less in a Spanish public. It is too strong, too delicate, and too profound for that; it would be vitiated and corrupted, misunderstood; and furthermore, *it does not need* this, for it is equally self-sufficient in the consciousness of one man as of two, or a thousand. It is undoubtedly bent toward being a public doctrine, but in *rational form* and by natural degrees, and in no other way.[15]

4

Toward a better world

1. Doctrine and utopia

The orbit traced by a militant doctrine results from the reciprocal action of two forces, one represented by the doctrine's inherent strength, its capacity for growth and development, and the other made up of the ideas and beliefs among which – and often against which – it becomes established. Hence there are two forms of dynamic energy which, with their constant attraction and repulsion, mark the shape and trajectory of a body of doctrine. If the ideas and beliefs prevailing at a given moment could be projected upon a flat surface, we would have an ideological map very similar to a political one. As in the latter, boundary lines would represent the more or less precarious balance between expansion and resistance. Doctrines, like individuals and nations, live 'agonically', in incessant conflict not only between being and non-being, but between being and wanting to be forever. Stretching Unamuno's analogy a little too far, perhaps, it might be said that to study the evolution of a doctrine is to write the history of its 'agony'.

A dual function, both defensive and offensive, can also be observed in every militant doctrine. The desire to persist and the intent to triumph occur simultaneously in such doctrines, except that any triumph, no matter how decisive it appears to be, is only the prelude to new struggle. From this perennial hand-to-hand fight no doctrine can emerge unscathed. First of all it must choose a tactic, and the adoption of a tactic already implies a tacit surrender to the pressure of circumstances. The position occupied by a doctrine on the spiritual chessboard of a period does not spring either from chance or free choice. The real determining factors of that position are the nature and strength of prevailing ideas and beliefs. The doctrine newly arrived on the scene must affirm its purposes by contrast with these, and to do so it must work out a plan of campaign. It must also attract allies, sometimes not the most desirable ones. It must willingly resign itself to contingency.

And lastly, it must abandon everything not strictly necessary for the defense or conquest of the objectives it has set itself.

Hence, if the evolution of a doctrine is examined step by step, it will be observed that there is a constant production of outgrowths and an equal process of elimination, both unmistakable signs of its progress through existence. A doctrine which does not show these changes must be thought of as non-viable, dead almost as soon as it emerged from its creator's brain; or, at most, as a utopian doctrine condemned to gravitate eternally, like a lifeless planet, beyond the faith of men. To regret that a body of doctrine has turned aside from its original path as it matured is a mark of ingenuousness that would be pardonable if it did not also indicate a supine ignorance of life and history. The only thing that does not turn aside from its original intention is utopia, and this is not strange, for utopia is precisely that which cannot be firmly attached to reality, and hence escapes the corrosive action of time and space. But every doctrine must contain a utopian component that acts like a compass needle, with whose aid the course is re-established when there is danger of losing it. Its value is merely corrective, no more, and it consists in keeping in sight the image of an ideal good, all the more tempting the more inaccessible it is. There is no better means of inciting man's enthusiasm than the hope of a happier world perpetually hidden beyond the horizon. But it would be a grave error to close one's ears to the urgent solicitations of real life in order to devote oneself to the sterile joys of a rational construction, as perfect as a geometrical figure and equally lifeless. The polestar guides the sailor, but is not his port of arrival.

2. The ideal of humanity

The utopian polestar used by Krausist doctrine to maintain a straight course was the *Urbild der Menschheit*, published in 1811, a preliminary work or, rather, a statement of the principles to which the later, more concrete and specialized work of Krause and his future disciples was to be adjusted. It would be well to stress the precise meaning of the word *Urbild* in this context. Krause maintains that humanity, as a voluntary determination of God, has been endowed from the beginning with the faculties needed to carry out the lofty and noble charge laid on it by its Creator. But man, the victim of ignorance, obduracy, and selfishness, has not succeeded in realizing his latent perfections. However, he has never completely lost the notion of his origin and destiny; and it is not strange that certain select individuals who possess a particularly robust intelligence or especially keen sensitivity have been able to discern, through the surrounding darkness, rays of light from that potential excellence and prophecies of mankind's future point of arrival. But with the advent of the scientific spirit and the primacy of reason, what was formerly the prerogative of a mere handful of men has become an almost universal aspiration. Humankind, says Krause, shows signs of turning away from its age-old alienation and is beginning to bend its steps toward universal solidarity, based on rational realization of the common dependence of all men and their subordination to God and divine laws. Placed in this context, the word *Urbild* acquires a dual meaning. On the one hand it means *archetype*, an original pattern; but on the other it has the same meaning as *teleotype*, the final form to be assumed by human solidarity.

There is no doubt that when Sanz del Río adapted Krause's most lucid and deeply felt book into Spanish, he had to wrestle with the problem of translating adequately this dual meaning of *Urbild*. He was not satisfied with *archetype* because he felt that, though it seemed to be the most appropriate word, it might easily lend itself to distorted interpretations. The word insinuated, in fact, an undesirable relationship with the Platonic notion of *idea* or transcendental image, of which the earthly thing is a deceptive and ephemeral copy. And Krause would have been the first to reject the possibility of such a link. The Platonic declaration that the universe of ideas constitutes the only authentic reality would have seemed inadmissible to him. According to Krause, humanity is God's free and supreme creation. As such it cannot be condemned to live in a perpetual state of hallucination and error, to grope its way through a world of phantoms; rather, humanity is in principle capable of achieving full consciousness of its origin, its faculties, and its eventual destiny. Harmonic rationalism rejects outright the myth of the cave. It is true that Krause admits human blindness, but he does not consider it innate or incurable. When God made man free and responsible, he made it possible for him to live either in truth or error. But he has also given man the gift of reason. If man does not let himself be guided by it, he runs the constant risk of going astray; and it must be remembered that, to the eyes of a Krausist, evil lies not in moral deviation but in ignorance of the spiritual legacy each man bears within himself. Hence reason is the seat of *rectitude*, in the dual sense of *integrity* and *discipline*. Only a man who molds his words and actions to the rational norm deserves to be called a whole man.[1]

It is not the idea in its Platonic meaning, that of a single genuine reality which, being sufficient unto itself, does not need to be realized in the sphere of concrete things, but the idea as a generative principle which 'contains within itself a world of secondary knowledge and applications. . . and which, scarcely has it gleamed in the spirit, wishes to be carried out in time and circumstances. . . and solicits and urges us insistently until it has become an effective reality':[2] this is the primary meaning of the Krausist *Urbild*. The formula of this generative principle is the following: 'Humanity is the harmonic synthesis of Nature and Spirit under the absolute unity of God.'[3] The Krausist philosophy's entire metaphysic gravitates around it. But it is obvious that the detailed elaboration of this principle could not be fitted into a small volume aimed at the reader unversed in philosophical matters. The more demanding reader could follow it step by step in Krause's other, more technical books. And by performing an act of violent simplification, Sanz del Río imitated his master by offering us that principle as previous to all experience, although it 'agrees in advance' with experience.[4]

The second meaning of *Urbild* is the realization in time of the aforesaid generative principle. In this stage the *idea* becomes an *ideal* or objective toward which rational will is aimed. Hence we are now dealing with a projected task or rule of conduct that will bring into effective existence what has previously been only pure concept.

When this idea of humanity is clear to the spirit and moves the spirit internally to change it into a fact, then directions and practical plans of action can be decided upon; that is, an ideal is formed as a response to the question: how should human relationships, the tendencies and directions contained within humanity, be arranged so that they will correspond to its nature and the fulfillment of its destiny?[5]

It was this plan of action which attracted Sanz del Río's attention very early in his studies and led him to give his adaptation of *Urbild der Menschheit* the title of *Ideal de la Humanidad para la vida*, deliberately accentuating the crusading flavor so obvious in the original. For tactical reasons he passed over the abstract part of Krausist doctrine for the moment, in order to concentrate his attention on the area of the eminently human, the sphere of moral problems and, still more concretely, the 'character and moral needs' of the Spanish people. Clearly the *Ideal de la Humanidad* had to be an adaptation made in accordance with the pattern best suited to the demands of a specific cultural psychology. 'It is not our intention, aimed for the present at building

rather than arguing,' announced Sanz del Río in the preface, 'to subject to close examination the principles which formed the basis of those
[Krause's] essays.'[6] At least on this occasion, the subtle reasoning and
peculiar nomenclature disappear. The work is humbly offered to the
public as 'an attempt at a practical philosophy, both individual and
social'. The urgent task is to rehabilitate life, to imbue it with meaning.
Values that have no other justification than routine or mere persistence
must be excluded from the new value structure. The disorientation
which so oppresses modern man springs from the fact that, having
ceased to believe in many of the ideas received from tradition, he has
not yet succeeded in mastering new forms of thought and action.
'In the unfathomable depths of moral freedom, in the world of intentions, in the sanctuary of conscience, in the higher sphere of first and
last purposes, vast, dark, and almost deserted regions lie before us today
where the inner voice does not speak, nor the spirit of good inspire us,
nor zeal for virtue reawaken us.'[7] Modern man swings between the two
poles, both deleterious, of cynical nihilism and the paroxysm of the
passions. Both states of mind are symptomatic of the 'poverty and
silence of the inner man'. Sanz del Río maintains that only philosophical reason, exhorting and supporting natural reason, is capable of
curing the illness that saps the energies of present-day humanity.
Philosophical rationalism constructs the one image of the world that
can be conceived of as universally valid. And in the preface to *Ideal de
la Humanidad*, where Krausist ethics is summarized, he plainly states
the need to return to a rationalism that will be severe with itself and
with its enemies both past and present: 'most men incline to be guided
by the easy current of someone else's dictates as the plainest and easiest
expedient for them, failing to realize that the necessary path, the only
dignified and safe path, consists in paying heed to the dictates of reason,
which illumines and guides all men and each man equally'.[8] This
Krausist pairing of reason and dignity is typical. Not to live in harmony
with a rational standard means resigning oneself to 'a humble and
voluntary moral servitude', to something, in short, incompatible with a
creature in whom the Creator has deposited the seeds of unlimited
power.

And it should be carefully noted that the overlordship of reason is
understood here as absolute overlordship. To place any obstacle whatever in reason's path means denying it in its entirety. Clearly alluding
to the Scholastics, Sanz del Río censures those who, though they accept
reason as the standard of life, do so only 'provided that it has the

sanction of faith', without which reason must 'halt its progress, make its voice fall silent, and renounce its own standards and law'. Sanz del Río condemns such subordination of reason to faith as contrary to natural law or, what for him amounts to the same thing, to divine law.

If the divine law of reason consists in investigating *discursively* the personal relationships of created beings and life, we would contradict this law and presumptuously correct its author by claiming that reason might on occasion, or for a strange irrational cause, leave this path and innate tendency which it has received from God himself, not from men or from any human authority.[9]

Sanz del Río inveighs with equal vigor against those students and practitioners of the natural and social sciences who proclaim the sterility of philosophical reason in their particular disciplines and campaign in favor of a radical empiricism, divorced from any theoretical formulation. To these people, the positivists, the Krausist leader replies that they should look around them and see how eminent contemporary naturalists and economists are turning to philosophy 'in order to provide a foundation for, generalize, and interrelate their respective sciences'. But even if this were not the case, could any science be cultivated without applying to it the fundamental ideas that only reason can supply?[10]

In the preface of *Ideal de la Humanidad*, therefore, a picture is drawn of the two chief adversaries against which the Spanish Krausist movement had to pit its forces. The first of these, Scholastic philosophy, represented the past. It was indeed the traditional and implacable enemy of 'pure' rationalism. The intellectual gymnastics of Balmes had succeeded in imparting a good deal of flexibility to the venerable school's tired muscles. But premature death cut off the author of *Filosofía fundamental* in mid-task, and most of the Catholic apologists who followed him preferred arguing to thinking. They made up for their lack of mental agility, however, with an excess of aggressive zeal. They could count on political support from traditionalists and ultramontanists, whose machinations were responsible for the inclusion of *Ideal de la Humanidad* in the Roman *Index*[11] and the persecution of Krausism in the universities. So it is no exaggeration to suggest that if Scholastic philosophy had been its only rival, Krausism would have won eventually. However, the school was so absorbed in the vicissitudes of this somewhat sordid battle that it either could not or would not realize that a new and fearsome enemy was coming up from behind: positivism, for which Krause's philosophy, like all idealist philosophy, represented an anachronistic relic. Strengthened by close links with the experimental sciences, the positivist school had announced, in the name of future philosophy, the death of metaphysics.[12] The Krausists' astonishment when they heard themselves stigmatized as retrograde – they, who had prided themselves on being in the vanguard of progress – contributed in large part to their feeble and inept defense. It was precisely the kind of attack for which they were unprepared. And it is a special paradox that at the very moment when they thought their triumph was sealed by the September Revolution, defections from the Krausist camp began. Either in the direction of neo-Kantianism or the natural sciences, many of the school's disciples began to go over to active participation on the side of positivism. And it is not strange that in mid-1875 so fervent a Krausist as Canalejas should confess that 'among the disciples of Don Julián Sanz del Río many varied and mutually hostile tendencies have appeared. A school no longer exists.'[13]

3. The schism in man

In leafing through *Ideal de la Humanidad* we find in Chapter IX of the Introduction an italicized question which dramatizes the importance conferred in advance on the possible reply: *Is there health for man?* The question is very far from being the simple caption used to mark off an academic proposition or indicate an intellectual pastime. In fact it is one more formulation of the anguished question man has been addressing to the four winds since time immemorial, often receiving no other answer than the ironic echo of the question itself. The use of the word *health* is especially apt here, for indeed the *Ideal* is a brief compendium of how to diagnose and treat the spiritual ailments that afflict the human condition.

Unamuno says of Descartes that he strikes a profoundly individual chord when he allows to burst through the placid surface of his rationalist logic, perhaps without meaning to, the desperate longing of the man who, beyond all philosophies, 'prétendait autant qu'aucun autre gagner le Ciel'. What this sentence reveals to us about Descartes's inner feelings is of inestimable value. Every philosophical system, Unamuno shrewdly suggests, eventually reduces itself to the *rationalization* of something whose origin is simply an inexpressible yearning or an irrational impulse.[14] In this view philosophy would be a way to evade the incurable torment that is human existence. So, from that selfsame torment arises the question, Is there health for man? And it can be said that all of Krausist philosophy arises from the desire to give a rational answer to that question. But, unlike other rationalist systems, Krause's does not attempt to blot out the traces of that impulse or yearning which are previous to any process of reasoning. 'Presentiment', 'intimate longing and yearning', and 'inclination of the spirit' play an important role in harmonic rationalism. When he speaks of the better world toward which present-day humanity is progressing as if drawn by a magnet, Sanz del Río lets these revealing words escape him: 'We... do not see this with our eyes; but we feel it more closely still, in our hearts and in the confidence that the mere idea of this ultimate pleni-tude gives to our present activities.'[15] But what are this inner feeling and intimate confidence for? Above all, they cause the individual not to feel, as he now feels, 'unprotected in the war that divides his heart today, and disconcerts it and causes it to despair...an alternation of shadow and light, of weakness and strength'.[16] In the second place, it impels him to act, to pour out his energy generously in activity that allows him to face his destiny, which is nothing but pure uncertainty. A man who is lost in the desert has no alternative, if he is to save himself, but to walk; to walk by following, if possible, a route prescribed by reason, but to walk in any case. Krause's philosophy is essentially a philosophy of action, for as one of his disciples has declared, 'all of life is action in the broad and rational meaning of the word'.[17]

Two champions, both of them powerful and at first glance irrecon-cilable, battle for men's hearts. One is the world of concrete things that is revealed to the senses. The infinite variety of physical reality, with its immediate evidence, invites man to squander his reserves of energy and will in actions all of which tend to decentralize him, to take him out of himself. In his ambitious and frantic desire to embrace the reality accessible to the senses, man forgets that when that reality is accepted in an undifferentiated way it is both inaccessible and a mere illusion. It is not life that he embraces, but 'the shadow of life'. The physical world, however, is not a formless maelstrom. 'Pure' nature – an essence, after all, whose origin is divine – is a delicate and extremely complex structure in which 'each thing seems to relate to other things of its own kind and to progress confidently toward its respective goal'.[18] Now, man's discovery of that subtle structure is precisely the rejection of sensorial evidence. The physical and mathematical laws that govern the world of the concrete are distilled, through the intellect, in frequent contradiction of the senses' dictates.

The second champion is 'pure' spirit, which exercises upon man an action contrary to that of the first. While nature exhorts the individual to come out of himself, 'spirit obliges him to withdraw into himself, to move away from contact with the life that smothers the purity of ideas'. Hence we are dealing with an exclusive world governed by laws of its own; a conceptual, aseptic world invulnerable to the damaging action of space and time: in short, a non-world. But note that when we say 'pure spirit', 'pure nature', we employ – and this is characteristic – the language spoken in that non-world. For it is idle to seek such purity in man, and if he can conceive it he does so only through abstraction. In the mind of God the human individual is neither pure spirit nor pure nature, but rather the synthesis in which the nature-spirit antithesis is resolved and transcended.

But alas, only in the mind of God. In historical reality 'man lives as if in an alien land, alternately in nature and spirit, and alternately cast first out of one realm and then out of the other. . .like an exile without a homeland or a home'. Is there health for man? Yes, but only when 'our humanity will be an inner kingdom everywhere in the world, a peaceful and harmonious *domesticity*', when 'the guardianship which, in past history, spirit and nature have alternately usurped' will be reduced, and when, finally, the human individual is, 'in fact as in idea, the synthesis where those two opposites come together in harmony, motivated by the law of divine unity in the world'. To those who might object that this was no more, after all, than a pious wish, Sanz del Río replied, 'We live in a closed time, and cannot anticipate historical reality; but from what we know up to now, this ultimate plenitude appears to be the constant purpose of the history we are in process of making, if it can be so expressed, on our own account and at our own risk.'[19]

4. Sociability and progress

Ideal de la Humanidad is divided into three sections: (a) humanity as archetype; (b) humanity as historical reality; and (c) humanity as universal aspiration. In general, this tripartite division corresponds to three different ways – metaphysical, historical, and ethical – of looking at the problem of human life.

In the first section the fundamental principles on which the whole argument is based are set forth. Among them the Krausist definition of man is paramount. Sanz del Río writes:

Man, the living image of God and capable of gradual perfection, must live in religion united with God and subordinated to God; he must carry out, in his limited place and sphere, the harmony of universal life, and show that harmony in a beautiful external form; he must come to know God and the world through knowledge; and he must, in the clear recognition of his destiny, educate himself.[20]

This definition bares the essential part of Krausist thought. Man is idea, insofar as he is 'the living image of God'; he is history, insofar as his evolution presupposes the gradual realization of that idea in time; and he is moral will, insofar as all his acts must guide him, 'in the clear recognition of his destiny', to live in harmony with himself, his fellow men, and his Creator.

In this description of man the forms of association that will be the object of special attention in the second section are already apparent: family, nation, state, science, art, religion. Each of them testifies, according to its nature, to the fact that 'this life has its definitive fulfillment only in social form'.[21] In each of them the desire to create a fundamentally human society is distributed historically. From the family, the primary form of association in which the germ of all the others is contained, to the grouping of states or ecumenical religions, it is possible to trace the progress of human sociability; a progress which, to be sure, does not exclude temporary regression, but whose general intent reveals the instinctive or reasoned belief in man that living means 'living in positive and harmonious relationship' with his fellow men. Indeed, this is the only meaning that Krausist philosophy attributes to *progress*. Progress and moral perfectibility are two different ways of expressing the same idea. Man progresses only in the measure in which he realizes that what is common to all men – humanity – obeys a single law and shares a single destiny. In short, progress will bring into being the moral perfection implicit in the idea of humanity.

It is hardly necessary to say that the transition from one form of association to another of greater scope does not mean that the form that has been surpassed had attained its maximum possible perfection. We need only look around us to realize that no form of association in existence today is even remotely perfect, for of none can it be said that, even within its own limited sphere, it has fulfilled the purpose for which it was created. The object of every form of association is to resolve the disparities and antagonisms of its parts in a higher harmony endowed with a substantivity of its own. A society, if it is to deserve the name, must be organic and must act with unity of purpose. Only then does it become *a social person* and, as is observed in the best essay written on the subject, 'every community of individuals – or societies – united to carry out a real purpose, or several purposes, or all purposes, through their mutual cooperation, constitutes an organism of its own, one substantially different from each of its members and even from the mere sum of those members'.[22] But divorce, the class struggle, war, and intolerance show by their persistence how defective is the present organization of marriage, the State, the nation, and religion. But if one thinks about it for a moment, there is no reason to be surprised by this. Man himself, who is ideally the synthesis of two antagonistic essences – nature and spirit – lives in reality suffering over his inability to harmonize them. And if he lives like this, there is nothing remarkable in the fact that the radical contradiction every man carries within himself infiltrates all of his associative creations. In short, no form of association existent today fulfills its ideal mission, for man, its creator, has not yet been able to resolve the struggle that goes on within himself.

Hence it is useless to try to perfect present forms of association without previously liquidating the contradictions that plague concrete man. Those who habitually proclaim the incurability of social ills, the militants of cynicism and the champions of systematic disillusionment, the nihilists and prophets of disaster, must be reminded that they are abdicating from their human condition, and that the root of the sickness does not lie in the family, or the State, or science, or religion, but within themselves, firmly planted in their individual consciousness. That organism of organisms which we call 'world' rests, for each individual, on his intuition of the unity of his own self. Strictly speaking, the Krausist world is nothing but a colossal projection of the intimate cohesion of nature and spirit which each man, no matter how little effort he expends, discovers in the depths of his own being. In every inquiry about the world, the individual has no choice but to start from himself and return to himself. For, in reality, he is the beginning and end of that inquiry, the beginning and end of all philosophy. What man urgently needs to do, therefore, is 'to educate himself... in the clear knowledge of his destiny', which in the last instance is the destiny of humanity as a whole. At every instant of his earthly life the human being must conduct himself as if the salvation or shipwreck of the entire human species depended on his acts. For the radius of man's – each man's – responsibility takes in 'the great globe itself'. The individual does not answer for himself to humanity so much as humanity answers for itself to God. 'As this idea becomes clearer... and this hope [that of a better world] firmer, the vacuum which all of us feel today, both inside and outside us, will disappear. . . and we will organize a new life with a prearranged social and individual plan.'

5. *Commandments of Humanity*

Sanz del Río describes the nature of this self-education in a series of precepts to which he gives the name of *Commandments of Humanity*, an inappropriate title from any point of view, since it is not to humanity considered as an abstract whole but to the human individual, to Tom, Dick, and Harry, that they are aimed. By moving in the direction of the concrete and prescriptive, Sanz del Río puts a personal stamp on Krause's thought, whose chief defect is its diffuseness and generalizing tendency. The Spanish philosopher's intent is clear. The book he is offering the public ought to contain, in addition to its speculative and vaguely desirable precepts, a series of practical suggestions, clearly and succinctly expressed so as to be understood easily by the ordinary reader. Hence *Commandments* attempts to summarize and codify the essential features of Krausist ethics. In it any question having to do with moral conduct receives a definite response.[23]

It is well known that *Commandments of Humanity* achieved greater fame than that of the book of which it formed part, as a kind of addendum or clarification. For the common reader it embodied the new philosphy's true meaning, as a sort of Ten Commandments which absolved the person who familiarized himself with them from any further exploration of Krausist doctrine. The rest of the book was relegated, except for a small minority, to the no-man's-land of the scholarly treatise. With the exception of these twenty-three articles, *Ideal de la Humanidad* was a book more respected than studied. More than one reader hastened over its theoretical arguments favoring a new ethics and went straight to the kernel, the clear and authoritative recommendation: 'You must do good with pure, free wholeness of will, and by good means'; 'You must affirm the truth only because, and insofar as, you know it, not because another knows it; without examination of your own self you must not affirm or deny anything at all.' This was certainly easy to understand, especially if the reader showed an aversion to prescriptive, probabilist, or empirical ethics, and was looking for an inflexible, unconditional, and absolute code of ethics, nourished entirely by the intrinsic validity of rational behavior. The reader doubtful of the truths of dogma or faith could find here a justification for free examination of conscience, for which there is no other truth than that which the individual discovers for himself through the effective use of his rational faculties. *Commandments* offers an excellent example of how Sanz del Río, even more than his teacher Krause, tried to clothe the rationalist structure of his thought with words that smacked of religion; but he did not do so to disguise that structure, rather to dignify it in the eyes of a public accustomed to hearing condemnations of every kind of rationalism untempered by faith and revelation. Despite the Biblical flavor of the word, however, these *Commandments* are not those of the law of God,[24] thundered out by a scowling Jehovah against the perverse and contumacious human race, but those of the *Law of Reason*, the orderer of chaos, dissipator of the shadows of error, source and object of all knowledge.

5

Germanophilia

1. Spain discovers Germany

With his studies in Germany during 1843 and 1844 Sanz del Río opened a period of incalculable importance in the history of modern Spanish thought, namely the period of discovery and exploration of German cultural values in their triple dimension: philosophical, literary, and scientific. To find something comparable in the intellectual life of another country we would have to think of the repercussions in France of Madame de Staël's German travels, or the influence in England of the Teutonic enthusiasms of Coleridge and Carlyle. Beginning with Sanz del Río, it is hardly possible to find a thinker or man of science in Spain who does not reflect, with greater or lesser intensity, some facet of the German spirit. Obviously Sanz del Río was only indirectly responsible for the later repercussions of his philosophical pilgrimage. He was very far from suspecting that, hidden among the folds of the doctrine he had brought from Germany, other bodies of doctrine had been smuggled in, as it were, and that these would eventually tear his doctrine to shreds and dissolve it away. But it is also true that, by developing under the influence of the intellectual interest aroused by Krausism, these other ways of thinking and acting bore witness, even long after they had supplanted it, to the foreign doctrine's extraordinary strength.

There is no doubt that the time was ripe for the germination of Germanophile seeds in Spain. As early as 1814, the date when Juan Nicolás Böhl de Faber published his *Reflexiones de Schlegel sobre el teatro*, there were signs of the increasing interest with which the Germans were studying and writing about Spanish letters, especially seventeenth-century drama. And once the scope of their enthusiasm was learned, Agustín Durán could declare that it was the Germans who had most accurately and carefully spread the knowledge of Spain's literary history. Durán was referring not only to the works of August Wilhelm

49

Schlegel, Jakob Grimm, and Friedrich Diez, but also to the fact that the first history of Spanish literature had been written by a German, Friedrich Bouterwek.[1] It was precisely during Sanz del Río's stay in Germany that C. A. Dorhn's collection of Golden Age plays was in course of publication,[2] and Emanuel Geibel's translation of Spanish ballads also saw print.[3] And a year after his return to Spain the first volume of Adolf von Schack's history of Spanish dramatic literature was published.[4]

It was not easy to accept without embarrassment the fact that foreigners were working hardest to make the Spanish people's literary creations known in Europe. But there was a strong element of gratitude along with the embarrassment. In the short space of half a century, the Germans had placed themselves in the forefront of enlightened Europe. And this cultured nation, with which Spain had scarcely had any recent material or intellectual commerce, was spontaneously taking on the task of doing justice to Spanish culture.[5] Against what? Against French classicism, against the French disdain for European national cultures and especially national literatures. Much time was to pass before it was understood that the German romantics' Hispanophilia, like their Anglophilia, was to some degree accidental, consisting of simple skirmishes in the general campaign to free German culture from French influence. German scholars and poets sought allies against the common enemy in Spanish and English letters, in an attempt to counteract effectively the French cultural expansion which, ever since the seventeenth century, had been reducing the richness and variety of the European spirit to a single mold. And this – it is not superfluous to note – happened at exactly the time when there was an attempt, through military coalitions, to halt the Napoleonic invasion of the Continent. The struggle against French cultural imperialism, transmuted into an intellectual battle, reproduced the struggle against the political and military imperialism represented by Napoleon. Shakespeare and Calderón did battle with Racine just as Wellington and Castaños fought Bonaparte.

The paradoxical part of all this is that the first news that filtered into Spain about German literature and philosophy came almost exclusively from French sources. In addition to Madame de Staël's famous book, the most important of these were Constant's comments on the German theater, Barante's translations of Schiller, Nodier's of Goethe, Loeve-Veimars' of Wieland, and Quinet's of Herder; this permitted a small group of Spaniards to acquire some idea of thought and letters beyond the Rhine. As for German philosophy, any curiosity that existed would have had to be satisfied with works of Gérando and Villers dating from the first decade of the nineteenth century, and later with other, more scholarly works by Rémusat, Ahrens, Bartholmès, Barchou de Penhoën, etc. 'There arrived in Spain,' writes Canalejas, 'like waves to the farthest shore of a very broad beach, a few sounds and murmurs of the German schools, arousing the fears and infatuations that the half-understood always brings; and it was at this point, on his return from his research trip to Germany, that Sanz del Río was appointed to the chair in Madrid.' The same author states – and no one could know it better than he – that 'beginning in 1857, and not before, taste and enthusiasm started to spread, not for Krausist philosophy but for German philosophy'.[6] The initial effect of Sanz del Río's lectures, therefore, was to lead his hearers' curiosity toward the region of German thought, a region all the more tempting because unexplored. For this purpose it was necessary to become familiar with the German language; and indeed, at that time a lively desire to learn it arose. However, the number of persons who were shipwrecked on the linguistic reef appears to have been very high.[7] Until the early years of the twentieth century there were very few Spanish intellectuals who knew German well. And in some cases, works as important as Mommsen's *History of Rome* and Duncker's *History of Antiquity* were translated into Spanish not directly from the original but through French translations.[8]

Hence we must place the beginnings of assiduous study of German culture by educated Spaniards in the ten years preceding the September Revolution. In philosophy, initial explorations were confined to the outstanding figures of idealism. Sanz del Río was to lecture extensively on Kant, Hegel, Fichte, Schelling, and Herbart from his university chair, even if his sole object was to prove that Krause's doctrine overcame the contradictions observable in the other systems. And so, what students at the University of Madrid knew about German philosophy was limited to notes taken in class or second-hand comment offered by one French publication or another.[9] Since they could not turn to the original texts of the philosophers mentioned (and impugned) in class, Sanz del Río's students had perforce to accept his judgments and hew to the Krausist doctrine, the only one that was explained amply, authoritatively, and systematically. It would be unjust to accuse Sanz del Río of this exclusivity. Although his preference for Krause was obvious in his lessons and writings, he was always especially careful not to impose his opinions as if they were articles of faith: 'It is not a question', he writes, 'of creating a doctrine or a school, something which in general I deplore as unsuitable to philosophy, and which I totally condemn and reject.'[10] He constantly advised those of his disciples who showed an interest in modern philosophy to learn German and discover the rich and stimulating German contributions for themselves. All the rest would be only a semblance of knowledge, false learning. And though there were very few who followed his counsels, this only shows that the period of active initiatives and intellectual adventure was yet to come.

2. *Wissenschaft* or science?

Besides importing the doctrine of one German thinker, Sanz del Río, 'standard-bearer of the Germanophiles in Spain', as one antagonist calls him,[11] made great efforts to acclimatize the German idea of science. And since, as we continue to deal with the intellectual history of the Krausist period, we often encounter the noun *ciencia* and the adjective *cientifico* applied in a sense different from the one they ordinarily have in Spanish, it will be well to explain this unusual application so as to avoid possible confusion.

The German idea of science? Yes. Though it is well known that in Spanish, as in other languages, the word *ciencia* had and still has more than one meaning, there is no doubt that during the apogee of Krausism it was given the peculiar meaning of the German word *Wissenschaft*. Before and after that time the Spanish word was equivalent to the French *science*; that is, it meant 'exact and reasoned knowledge of certain specific things'. In imitation of its French counterpart the Spanish word expanded, on the one hand, to include areas of knowledge of somewhat dubious exactness – 'political sciences', 'moral sciences' – and on the other it contracted, also by means of adjectives, to serve the quantitative or experimental disciplines – 'exact sciences', 'natural sciences'. But it has never been customary either in French or Spanish to include philosophy among the sciences. However, not only is philosophy included in the German *Wissenschaft*, it is the very heart of its meaning. And around philosophy are grouped studies such as jurisprudence, theology, and medicine, which were considered scientific only in Germany. *Wissenschaft* is the single and total structure of human knowledge. And it is exclusively in this sense that Sanz del Río and his disciples used the Spanish word *ciencia*.

Fichte was the most influential exponent of this unitary idea of science, which really began with Leibniz and had always enjoyed broad acceptance in Germany. It is significant that Fichte should have baptized his system with the name of *Wissenschaftslehre*, or Theory of Science; and this, in view of the purely speculative nature of Fichte's philosophy, is incomprehensible to anyone who equates science with the quantitative and empirical. According to Fichte, all science is articulation or system, and all scientific propositions converge in one fundamental proposition which in its turn unites them all. Krause was a pupil of Fichte's in Jena in 1797–1799, and eventually adopted an interpretation of science very similar to that of his teacher. Indeed, it was sufficient simply to confer an objective and absolute value on the fundamental unifying proposition, to build it into a *Wesen*, for the chief differences between the two philosophers to vanish. Krause's faithful follower Sanz del Río proclaimed in his turn that 'the object and ultimate aim of science is one', and that it is sufficient to examine carefully the boundaries that nominally exist between the disciplines included in science to observe that 'differences are lost in the unity which presides over them all'.[12] Sanz del Río, in conformity with the German idea of *Wissenschaft*, includes in this interpretation of science not only the exact, physical, and natural sciences, but also medicine, philosophy, theology, literature, history, law, and politics. Philosophy occupies the pre-eminent place:

In this fundamental organism, each and all of the sciences start from a basic principle leading to knowledge of a law or general formula, and with reference to this formula they compare and order these laws until they discover the common law that presides over particular ones, at which point philosophy, applying to all [the sciences] the unifying activity of the spirit in induction, deduction, and construction, gives them a faithful resemblance to the organism that is the world.[13]

Although this concept is found, either expressly or tacitly, in all the adherents of Krausist doctrine, it was Francisco Giner de los Ríos who described it most carefully. His essay entitled *Condiciones del espíritu científico* merits careful reading as a sample of the principles that govern the Krausist idea of science and scientific research.[14] Giner states as a fundamental law that 'knowledge in its absolute plenitude constitutes science and its reflective and systematic elaboration constitutes scientific investigation',[15] and adds that scientific knowledge does not differ from common knowledge because of its object, but because of its quality. Both modes of knowledge can be true, but while common knowledge contents itself with empirical evidence, scientific knowledge demands 'proved, sure, certain truth, authentically evident to us as truth, and capable of eliciting continuous and systematic testimony; that is, which continues to be confirmed step by step, without interruption, until it becomes the foundation of all proof, where it remains forever firm and valid'.[16] In this respect it is well to recall that the Krausists identified epistemology with metaphysics. Science is the full knowledge of reality; the basic reality is God and basic knowledge is knowledge of God; partial or adjectival aspects of reality which become material for special knowledge derive from God and are contained in God.[17] Hence science, like all reality, is a delicately articulated system 'where each part, only in its proper place in the whole and in its gradual relationships with the rest, possesses its own meaning and can be properly studied and known'.[18] So that in science there are three consecutive phases which compel the true man of science: (a) 'to argue, first of all, the whole problem of knowledge (*Logic and General Doctrine of Science*), whose eternal ideal must constantly preside over his subsequent investigations'; (b) 'to investigate the supreme principle of reality, upon which it is all founded and explained (*Metaphysics*)'; and (c) 'to explore, lastly, the organism in which that same reality displays, adequately and in ordered fashion, its unlimited inner variety (*Encyclopaedia*) and without which it is impossible for him to determine the concept, relations, place, value, and most necessary relationships of its object'.[19] Multiplicity in unity; this sums up the idea of science proposed by Giner.[20] It is, in fact, the ideal that prevailed in Germany early in the nineteenth century, when under the influence of Kant and Fichte it was believed that a single method is valid for all branches of knowledge, with the additional advantage that unity of method guarantees the unity, universality, and integrity of genuine knowledge. Strictly speaking it is not a scientific but a philosophical ideal, one that was already in crisis when Sanz del Río studied in Heidelberg and continued to lose ground during the second half of the century, with the increasing supremacy of the sciences of observation and experimentation.[21]

3. Krausist idea of the university

The idea that knowledge is an organic whole, and that its essential unity must preside over all scientific activities, was characteristic of Germany and resulted in large measure from the evolution and peculiar organization of that country's universities. The multitude of small states, the rivalries and emulations among them, religious differences, all favored the establishment of numerous university centers, many of them in very small towns. On the other hand, linguistic unity, the similarity of aims and ideals, and the aspiration of educated people toward political unification, tended to create close ties among teaching institutions.[22] Hence each university was a precinct where scholars lived and worked in mutual dependence, as well as a point of connection in the extensive network of centers of high scholarship that covered the face of the Germanic world. Over and above the political frontiers that separated them, the German universities forged the country's intellectual unity. 'It would be difficult', writes J. Conrad, 'to find among the different parts of Germany a stronger link than that offered by the universities, and in no other respect have the barriers dividing the states been broken down so long ago.'[23] The idea of *Wissenschaft* arose and developed from the physical multiplicity and spiritual unity of the German university system. It was presided over by administrative decentralization and the principle of academic freedom. The atmosphere in which it flourished was the narrow compass of a small town where each professor followed closely his colleagues' studies and research and took over whatever part of them he could use in his own work. Its ideal was the consideration of human knowledge as something objective, different from its cultivators, who were not thought of as 'creators' but only as 'servants' of science, in whose name they must renounce all personal or utilitarian considerations. Its ultimate aim was that of cooperating with other university centers in the construction of a national science which, in its turn, would be part of universal science.

In the long run, the outstanding characteristics of the German university were reduced to two – freedom and organic unity – and both these traits were totally absent from Spanish universities in Sanz del Río's time; yet he believed them indispensable for the future reform of advanced studies. He wrote from Heidelberg in 1844:

It must not be thought that *university* is, and means, the same thing in Germany as it does in Spain. Our universities are institutions where science is taught, formerly under the influence and even effective, direct, and intimate guidance of the Church, and now of the State; in Germany the university is, within itself and even in its teaching, an institution totally independent of both Church and State; provided that what is taught is truly science, neither State nor Church has legitimate action or intervention there...precisely this freedom is the basis of the life and prosperity in which this institution exists in Germany.[24]

From that time forward Sanz del Río never ceased to promote the cause of the autonomous university, as sovereign in its own sphere as Church or State in theirs, but a co-participant with them and other forms of association in working out a fundamentally human society. His disciples, without exception, were zealous defenders of freedom of teaching as opposed to the interference of public authority, either in the guise of protection or outright supervision. Giner de los Ríos believed that the time had come for the university to seek support in the society itself which it would have to serve and not in the State which had maintained it, and still maintained it, in a state of undignified vassalage.[25] Azcárate thought that the university's independence and vitality were closely linked, and declared that any institution given over to outside governance was rendered incapable of effective action.[26] And Salmerón held the view that a university center should have no other law than 'the free search for, and profession of, truth', and that, since this was an exclusively social aim, the teaching institution should be held responsible only to society.[27]

The September Revolution added to its reform program the principle of freedom of instruction as well as the inviolability of the teaching profession, and in conformity with both principles cancelled all the restrictive decrees of 1866 and 1867.[28] In the name of the Provisional Government, the Minister of Public Works, Manuel Ruiz Zorrilla, proclaimed in the decree of 21 October 1868 that 'instruction is free on all its levels and whatever its kind'. The chief advisers for the new directions in teaching were Sanz del Río and his followers. He himself was offered the rectorship of the University of Madrid, an offer he declined, accepting instead the deanship of the Faculty of Philosophy and Letters. But the rectorship of the University of Madrid went to Fernando de Castro, whose ideas of the teaching institution under his charge came directly from his close friend and collaborator Sanz del Río. The university was to become a free society of servants of the one and universal science, for the benefit of humanity. In the Circular sent by Castro on 20 November 1868 to the rectors of all Spanish universities both in the peninsula and overseas, he stated that 'all science [must] show its free character and a life of its own in a real, fundamental society which teaches, propagates, and applies it to the facts as an organic science in harmony with the order of the world and of history'. The preamble to the Decree of 21 October 1868 leaves no room for doubt with respect to the origin of the doctrine that has inspired it: 'One of the most persistent obstacles to the circulation of new ideas', it says, 'has been the monopoly of instruction. The State's scientific establishments have believed that they possessed the whole truth, and have regarded with disdain anything that did not fit into the framework of received formulas.' As a remedy, there was a call for the opening of teaching centers that would be free from the supervisory action of the State; it was hoped that these, through the competition they would offer to state schools, would help to raise the level of instruction in general and public instruction in particular. Further, it was announced that the State would offer facilities to anyone, not a member of the university professorate, who would like to 'make his aptitudes known and contribute to fomenting useful knowledge', and it was stated in passing that 'such professors, who should not have an appointment or salary from the state, have performed very important services for their country in Germany'. Hence the German *Privatdocent* system was accepted in principle. A quarter of a century had passed since Sanz del Río, in despair over the condition of Spanish universities and enthusiastic about German ones, had written to Revilla from Heidelberg:

As for what application can be found in Spain for the good elements of the German systems, I will say from the outset that, in general, there is none, or that the results would be bad rather than good. It would be necessary to begin by removing the innumerable obstacles, not only legislative but even political and social, which, in our country's public life...make it impossible for science to become a free and independent element in public life.

Now the September Revolution had removed the legislative obstacles, but that was all. The German-style university the Krausists had dreamed of was never more than a beautiful plan. But even though it was swept away by reactionary ire in the first years of the Restoration, the Krausist theory of education became the real basis for the liberal reforms introduced by Minister Albareda in 1881.

4. José del Perojo

Before the Franco-Prussian War, what was known in Spain about German cultural contributions was limited to philosophy and, to a lesser degree, literature. Even in the philosophical sphere such knowledge was incomplete, which did not prevent the Krausists from uttering opinions as premature as they were ill-considered. In the foreground of this peculiar perspective rose the towering figure of Krause; behind him, and dwarfed by him, appeared Kant and Hegel; and far back and out

of focus, Fichte, Schelling, and a few other proponents of idealism
could be discerned. Some notions of post-Hegelian philosophy and the
state of German science at mid-nineteenth century could be gleaned
from French publications, but these few glimpses were no longer
sufficient to satisfy the appetite for intellectual communication with the
lands beyond the Rhine. Precise information was needed about
philosophers like Schopenhauer and Hartmann, who were frequently
and extensively dealt with in French reviews. It was suspected that,
within German philosophy, they had made the transition from the
rational and abstract to the vital and concrete. There was a desire to
know more about the work of the cultivators of inductive and experimental science like Helmholtz, Wundt, Moleschott, Virchow, Fechner,
and especially Haeckel. Spanish interest in the theory of evolution
derived from the latter's comments on Darwin rather than directly
from the English naturalist. Articles on scientific subjects published
during the revolutionary period from 1868 to 1874 give us hints of the
subtle change that took place in Spain's intellectual climate as the last
quarter of the nineteenth century began. Rationalist philosophy and
dedication to deductive science – *Wissenschaft* – were giving ground to
positivism and the consequent enthusiasm for experimental and inductive science.

A young Cuban, José del Perojo y Figueras (1852–1908), contributed
vigorously toward accelerating this change. He had founded in Madrid,
late in 1875, the *Revista Contemporánea*, with the fundamental aim of
bringing into Spain and acclimatizing there the newest manifestations
of the German intellectual movement. It would be somewhat ingenuous
to assign to one man the shift of interest described above. But this does
not prevent us from regarding Perojo, as most of his contemporaries
did, as the leader of those who, intrigued by 'modern' German thought,
began to look askance at the 'outdated' Krausists. In order to understand the shift of which we speak, words saturated with political significance must be used. Before 1868 the Krausists and quasi-Krausists
had formed the nucleus of what might well be called Spanish intellectual *progressivism*. But after the Restoration the same could not be
said of them. The description 'progressivists' went to the proponents of
positivism, neo-Kantianism, Spencerian evolutionism and, very especially, to those who worked in the natural sciences. Strictly speaking
nobody regarded the Krausists as *reactionaries*. But they were regarded
as *outmoded*. They were not up-to-date, they did not march in the
'vanguard of thought'. And, naturally, no defect was greater than this

when the most urgent task was that of synchronizing Spain, spiritually and materially, with the rest of Europe.

Young José del Perojo was bold, iconoclastic, and ambitious. Like Sanz del Río he had studied philosophy in Heidelberg. His favorite teacher was Kuno Fischer, who preached a return to Kant, to a criticism stripped of the adiposities with which the metaphysicians of idealism had disguised it. Fischer was particularly concerned with the problem of reconciling philosophy and contemporary science; that is, the science of observation and analysis, a reconciliation that he believed was urgently needed if philosophy was to be more than arid verbalization or intellectual pastime. By this viewpoint Fischer emphasized the fact that only Kantian criticism, as a strict theory of knowledge, could take over the aspirations of science by channeling them. All metaphysical speculation must be excluded. The 'thing-in-itself' was a useless concept, a vestige of anachronistic 'substances' or 'essences'. The philosopher's attention, like that of the scientist, must be placed on the simple phenomenon, in the area of the knowable, for only there could philosophy and science collaborate and make each other fruitful. In short, Kuno Fischer was attempting to interpret Kant's philosophy by frankly positivist standards.

With this background, and convinced in addition that no contemporary nation could equal Germany in 'development and progress of thought', Perojo came to live in Madrid just before the Restoration. The Krausist movement was in full swing, and its chief centers of dissemination were the Athenaeum and the University of Madrid. But signs of cooling off had begun to appear in some members of the school. The indisputable ascendancy achieved by the doctrine after the September Revolution had brought with it a sort of relaxation of the old discipline and a perceptible diminution of faith in the virtues of harmonic rationalism. It was under these circumstances that Perojo struck up a friendship with Manuel de la Revilla, whom he caused without much effort to break with the Krausist school and enlist under the banner of neo-Kantianism. Through Revilla he also met two physicians, Drs Simarro and Cortezo, both of whom were interested in Comte's ideas.[29] Neo-Kantians and positivists formed a tacit alliance against Krausism and, after the middle of 1874, began to recruit followers among the younger members of the Athenaeum. Sanz del Río's disciples, still invulnerable within the University of Madrid, paid little attention to other fronts, and their ascendancy suffered an irreparable setback during the latter months of 1874. The official persecution of the early months of 1875 merely delivered the *coup de grâce* to an ideological body that had already received a mortal blow.

On 21 March 1875 Perojo fired the first barrage of print at the Krausists, in the form of an article entitled *Kant y los filósofos contemporáneos*, the first in a series of *Estudios sobre Alemania*.[30] In the article its author reviewed the multitude of schools and variety of directions that had replaced the philosophical systems of the first third of the century in Germany. What seemed to be the result of the dissolution and anarchy of German thought was deemed by Perojo to be quite the opposite, a sure sign of vitality and fertility. According to him the only thing that was inert and sterile was the unity proposed by previous systems and the exclusiveness of those thinkers who, claiming supreme truth for themselves, accused all other philosophies of being false. Kant's chief virtue was that he had fostered an atmosphere favorable to all forms and expressions of thought, even the most abstruse and apparently contradictory ones. In contemporary German philosophy, said Perojo, 'this or that particular system does not exercise hegemony over the truth, but philosophy is a real occupation, people think and work, and all or nearly all of them reject those intellectual leading strings, suitable for infantile temperaments, called Hegelianism, Fichteanism, or Krausism'.[31] The idealistic schools were out-of-date. Abandoned by really first-rate philosophers, they still served as a solace for old-fashioned thinkers and as support for the inept. But what was truly intolerable, the writer believed, was that the followers of Hegel or Krause, motivated by arrogance or ignorance, considered that other, more recent manifestations of philosophical thought were foolish or incomplete.

This first study, though weak as an attempt to prove that nineteenth-century German philosophy was nothing but the step-child of Kantian criticism, sufficed to make Perojo thought of, from that time forward, as extremely well-read in modern German thought, and as the person best equipped to introduce it into Spain. In particular, the bibliography that accompanied the article was very impressive. Its openly declared aim was to guide those readers willing to plunge into the thicket of mid-nineteenth-century German books and authors. Recently published works by Erdmann and Zeller, Hartmann and Fischer, Helmholtz and Virchow, Lotze and Wundt, demonstrated the ease with which, according to a contemporary critic, Perojo moved among 'the latest [German thinkers] who have appeared, those who are appearing, and even those who are still studying in the universities'.[32] It was the first bibliography of its kind published in a Spanish periodical of general circulation. To be sure, its usefulness was limited to those who knew the German language. But even so it served as an initial encouragement for more than one sally into the intellectual movement to which it bore witness.

Before being published in book form[33] Perojo's essays on intellectual life in Germany were printed, at short intervals, in the *Revista Europea* between 21 March and 8 August 1875. The study on Kant was followed by others on Heine, on Schopenhauer and philosophical pessimism, on the development of the natural sciences, on historiography and politics. To pause to examine the content of these articles lies outside the scope of this book. For our purposes it will suffice to state that they are all informative essays which, precisely because they are so, contain a tacit invitation to the reader to seek for himself broader and more precise information on the matters with which they deal. Perojo skillfully avoids both overspecialization and pedantry. His aim is not to explain difficulties away but to remove obstacles, suggesting here and there a path to be explored, citing some authorized text or providing clarifying examples. The intellectual route he follows takes him further and further away from the Krausists. They praised the advantages of withdrawal from the world, there to reflect systematically on a truth – better still, *the* truth – which they had grasped once and for all, and before which all the would-be solutions of philosophy and religion had to bow. But for the young Germanophile, 'systems. . . are molds that enclose and enslave; with them, thought loses spontaneity'.[34] He believed that what was needed to place Spain in harmony with Europe was not the solution proposed by the Krausists – that is, replacing one orthodoxy with another – but that the Spanish mind must be opened to the four points of the compass and exposed to diametrically contrasting currents of thought. Early in the Restoration Perojo undertook a task which offers striking similarities to that assumed several decades later by Ortega y Gasset. Perojo believed that the task of spiritual renewal demanded, as a start, close familiarity with what had been done and was being done in Europe; and for him Germany was the heart of nineteenth-century Europe, just as France had been its heart in the previous century. And if philosophical systems were somewhat in eclipse in Germany, and rather than making philosophy there was an attempt to see if it could be saved by allying itself with science, nothing was more puerile and anachronistic than to cling to a system as the Krausists had done, and to try to acclimatize it in Spain to the exclusion of all others. Systems, according to Perojo, are the infancy of philosophy. Only when philosophy sponsors free investigation can it be said that it has reached adulthood. The possibility of a truly Spanish philosophy demanded, in the first place, very careful study of the prevailing schools. But this was not enough. It would also be necessary to enter into the spirit of contemporary science,[35] to foster scientific work through establishment of suitable institutes where the best minds in Spain could gather, unprejudiced and untrammeled. Science without philosophy is simply a heap of unconnected data. Philosophy without science is barren wordmaking. During the few years when Perojo, in collaboration with Manuel de la Revilla, edited the *Revista Contemporánea*, the inexhaustible riches of contemporary European thought were spread before the Spanish reader's eyes. When the young Cuban's enemies accused him of Hispanophobia they were simply exaggerating, in their irritation, something that when looked at more dispassionately was only a desire to obtain a new and more accurate perspective. Doubtless his review did pay a great deal of attention to things foreign. But on the other hand almost all – not to say all – the other periodical publications overemphasized domestic affairs. And so there was a need for a watchtower from which to scan the far distance, gazing first at one sector of the horizon and then another. Leaving out of consideration factors of time and quality, it can be said that the *Revista Contemporánea*, taken all in all, was for the Spain of the Restoration what the *Revista de Occidente* was for the dictatorship of the nineteen-twenties. Both chose chiefly, though not exclusively, to inform and comment upon contemporary German thought. Moreover, one finds on reading Perojo that he anticipates certain opinions of Ortega's. He said in one article:

We want to be spectators of things, studying and investigating them, without making them into utilitarian means for life...The idea that science is the master of life is very deeply rooted, but this conviction, false...because life is much more than what science is capable of grasping...will disappear little by little, and in its place will come the disinterested love that science deserves...today, our ideal in science is the love of knowledge, love of the truth because it is the truth, and not out of mere utility or convenience.[36]

6

Gallophobia

1. Extent of French cultural influence

Closely linked to the intellectual Germanophilia introduced and fostered by the Krausist movement in Spain was another, completely different attitude: that of disdain, and at times of open aversion, toward the forms of French culture. It must be noted that this negative attitude obeyed historical and psychological impulses whose effect it is difficult to assess, though there is no doubt that it was considerable. There are many discrepancies to be observed in the idea that Spain formed of her neighboring country; and consequently no statement, however circumstantial, can explain and resolve those discrepancies. Geographic proximity is a source of close relationships as well as frictions. French cultural superiority lent itself to both admiration and envy. The triumphs of French arms and letters invited reflection on the bitter evidence of Spanish decline and the evocation, by contrast, of past times of splendour and influence. Those Spaniards who, in thrall to the prestige of their trans-Pyrenean neighbor, adopted French modes of thought and action came to regard their compatriots as closed-minded and hostile to progress and enlightenment. Spanish cultural nationalists, in their turn, accused the 'Frenchifiers' of being renegades and traitors who were plotting the annihilation of national identity and – who knows? – even the destruction of Spain's political independence. Breezes of freedom blew from France, but France was also the source of the vassalage imposed first by Napoleon's armies and then by those of the Duke of Angoulême. Though she continued to call Golden Age Spanish dramatists 'uncultured', France took over, and immortalized after her own fashion, subjects which those same playwrights had immortalized in theirs. The list of contradictions, both real and apparent, could be prolonged indefinitely. In any case, France presents a paradoxical face to Spain.

We have already referred to the true intentions of German romanticism, which were somewhat less disinterested than they appear at first glance.[1] But this is unimportant. Disregarding second intentions, what remains is the encouragement the German romantics gave Spaniards to assert their own tradition in opposition to the imperialism of French classicism. But unfortunately this call for the defense of cultural integrity did not reach the ears of most Spanish literary men and critics for nearly half a century. French classicism was at last exterminated in the peninsula, but not by the native genius, employed in the study and evaluation of its vernacular creations; rather, it was expelled by romanticism... French romanticism. The 'liberals' in literature – to use Victor Hugo's definition of the romantics – fought the 'reactionaries' of classicism in Spain with arguments and methods copied from their French counterparts; just as, in politics, the liberals of the Cortes of Cádiz in 1812 attacked the conservative faction, which was opposed to limitation of the monarch's power, with arguments lifted from the Declaration of the Rights of Man. Neither the Spanish War of Independence nor the struggle between classicists and romanticists succeeded in breaking Spain's cultural servitude with regard to France:

those who boasted of being most enlightened went on scorning our literature openly and calling it barbarous, judging our arts at much less than their true value, and denying any importance to our sciences and our philosophy. The submission, the vassalage, the obedience of Spaniards to France had no such counterparts at the time, in the intellectual sphere, as [the battles of] Bailén or Zaragoza or Gerona or the Second of May.[2]

However, every attempt at emancipation was condemned to failure from the outset unless it began by defining the French spirit and what was essential and characteristic about its cultural forms. Intellectual, literary, artistic, and social closeness with France dated from the early years of the eighteenth century. More than enough time had passed, therefore, to have blotted out completely the dividing line between the two cultures and amalgamated native and foreign elements. In a few select individuals like Feijoo, Cadalso, Forner, or Larra it is possible to study, not without uneasiness, the extreme to which this amalgamation had taken place in the area of cultural psychology. And it must be borne firmly in mind that we are talking about men whose adoption of French ideas had not led to an attenuation of their deep-rooted Spanishness. The same cannot be said of some of their more pedestrian countrymen. Each, according to his temperament, sought in French culture the spur that would rouse his own culture out of its long lethargy.

Nothing could undermine the prestige enjoyed in Spain by French culture until the intelligent Spaniard discovered other aspects of European thought. It was useless for a few fervid cultural nationalists to complain that immoderate enthusiasm for everything French was harmful, that it corrupted the very substance of the Spanish genius without, however, succeeding in placing Spanish creations on an equal plane with those of France. Motivated by fear of denaturalization, the cultural nationalists came perilously close to proposing total isolation. All ears had to be closed to the Gallic siren's insidious song. But those who shared this opinion were never more than a small minority. The reasonably well-educated Spaniard was convinced that his country had squandered her former strength, that irresistible impulse that had given Spain the primacy of the Western world in the sixteenth century. And he perceived, moreover, that the weakness was general, that it affected all aspects of national life and not only the spheres of intellect or art. Along with the loss of political and military pre-eminence, the Spaniard appeared to have lost confidence in his nation's abilities, not merely to achieve ambitious projects but simply to preserve a respectable position in the concert of European nations.

2. Prejudice against French philosophy

There was an important difference between the Gallophobia of the cultural nationalists and that which began to take shape with Sanz del Río. The former were xenophobes rather than Gallophobes, and if their aversion was chiefly aimed at French culture it was because, at the time, French culture had the primordial if not exclusive influence in Spain. They did not hate everything French simply because it was French, but because it was foreign; and undoubtedly their attitude would have been identical if the influential culture had been Italian or English instead of French. The Gallophobia of the Krausist leader and a goodly number of his disciples, however, arose from their conviction that the culture of France, when its principal ingredients were carefully analyzed, was harmful to the Spanish genius. Consequently, when they opposed it they did so not out of exaggerated nationalism, but convinced that the exclusive predominance of French cultural fashions would destroy the possibility of receiving a stimulus from some other foreign culture which might arouse the exhausted national spirit. And so it was a reasoned and analytical anti-Gallicism. Sanz del Río had already declared, after his interview with Victor Cousin, that he thought the scientific and philosophical aspects of French culture were 'deceptive and pure appearance', capable only of attracting frivolous and mundane minds.[3] Like Amiel and Constant, both fierce critics of the French mind,[4] the Spanish philosopher was irritated by the desire for public recognition, bordering on exhibitionism, displayed by so many intellectuals in the neighboring country. It does not require a great effort of imagination to guess that, in Sanz del Río's opinion, the chief defect of the French mind was its horror of intimate contact. Moved by this horror, the Frenchman flees from the human need to commit himself – a need proclaimed by Pascal, who, precisely because he did so, is the least 'French' of French thinkers – *s'engager*, as we would say nowadays, to an intellectual adventure which does not offer an unequivocal means of escape. This lack of human depth makes the Frenchman the archetypical extrovert. All speculation, sifted through his mind, slides toward the social dimension, as if he were convinced that the final validity of an idea depends on the degree of acceptance conferred on it by the majority of people. In philosophy as in the theater, Sanz del Río would have said, the French thinker measures success with the yardstick of public applause. To a man as modest as the Krausist leader nothing could have seemed more contrary to intellectual decorum than the French mind's desire to advertise itself. Rightly or wrongly, he believed that the popularity to which the French thinker aspired perverted the very foundation of truth – that is, of inner cohesion and harmony between the thinker and what he thinks – on which all philosophical speculation must be based. And he also suspected that this perversion arises from a special characteristic of French thought, namely its insidious quality of being easily grasped. Indeed, to obtain the approval he deems necessary, the French thinker is forced to reduce the most complex questions to clear language, easily accessible to the ordinary man; a language which, polished by a long tradition of classical simplicity and circumspection, does not tolerate arcane names for things or the complex syntactical patterns of modern philosophy, that is, of philosophy made in Germany. But technical language is not the only thing the French philosopher feels it necessary to eliminate in presenting his thought. To make it immediately comprehensible he must also sacrifice the cloudy area, translogical rather than logical, which surrounds what he has thought: uncertainty, anguish, the pain which, as in physical birth, accompanies the birth of a profoundly original thought. 'Never a cry of passion', writes Unamuno of Anatole France. 'It is not tragic skepticism; rather, it seems to be a comfortable passion, in order not to commit oneself seriously to the fire of life. And furthermore, all that about *tout comprendre, c'est tout pardonner*, to understand everything is to forgive everything, requires a correction, and it is that to understand everything is not really to understand anything.'[5] And this very characteristic statement of Unamuno's about Anatole France and, through him, about French *littératisme*, would have had Sanz del Río's hearty agreement, only he would have aimed it at Victor Cousin and his *philosophisme*. The Krausist leader's grave mistake was to think of the amiable professor at the Sorbonne as an incarnation of the Gallic spirit's cold superficiality. And this more than anything else demonstrates how great was his ignorance of all things French.

Sanz del Río's Gallophobia undoubtedly has very deep emotional roots. It contains a bit of national pride wounded by the aping of everything French and a good measure of nonconformity as well. But there is also an ethical ingredient, perhaps the most important one; something of that indefinable suspicion with which the man of puritanical moral principles views the products of a brilliant civilization. Paris, the capital of France, is the new Babylon, sensual and radiant, capricious and cruel as an expensive courtesan, before whose cleverly heightened charms the whole world bows in servile adoration. The fact that Sanz del Río confines his disapproval to the area of philosophical and scientific thought means only a change of tactics. The problem is now posed on intellectual grounds. The Krausist leader's intention is to show that philosophical thought, which he considers as the most noble, disinterested, and revealing facet of a culture, determines and explains the form and content of other cultural manifestations. He does not believe that French philosophical thought is superficial because all of French culture suffers from congenital superficiality, but that the culture of France is all superficial because the thought from which it is nourished lacks adequate substance.[6]

In view of all this, Sanz del Río contended that it was a serious mistake to offer homage to French science and philosophy. Both were the polished product of a people whose 'character', as Amiel says, 'is formal; that is, frivolous and material, or better still, artistic and not philosophical; because what it seeks is the outline, the style and manner of things, and not their inner life, their soul, their secret'. It was very important not to allow oneself to become depressed about the inferiority, in matters of the intellect, of Spain in comparison with France. That inferiority was more apparent than real. What Spain needed was to awaken the energies that lay dormant within her, to discipline them strictly and guide them in the direction indicated by the new ideal of humanity. Imitation of everything French, declared Sanz del Río, 'is all the more lamentable...when I think today that the qualities of spirit in our country are infinitely superior, in depth and consistency, to those of the French, without on the other hand degenerating into useless abstraction, as in Germany'.[7]

3. Scorn for French letters

Sanz del Río's disciple Francisco Giner followed a direction similar to his; he assumed the task of spreading the new anti-French attitudes to an area which, unlike the field of philosophy, immediately attracted the cultured reader's attention: the area of literary history and criticism. Giner's Gallophobia took shape in an essay written in 1862, under the title *Consideraciones sobre el desarrollo de la literatura moderna.*[8] This rather vague heading covers a number of quite shrewd observations on the French character, in the measure in which it is reflected in literary creation. It is not, therefore, French literature as *literature*, but as *psychology*, which primarily interests Giner. In his study literary data are analyzed as symptoms which, when skillfully put together, will permit a psychic portrait of the French nation. To do this Giner calls to his aid the Krausist idea of history. We have already seen that Krause carefully distinguished between two ways of interpreting history, arising, respectively, out of interest in what a people does – social and political, or external history – or in what it thinks and feels – history of 'ideas' in the broad sense, or internal history. It will also be recalled that Krause believed that only the second of these two modes was the true one.[9] And in identical vein, Giner asks the historian to do all he can to reach the deepest level of a nation's psychology, disdaining as insubstantial, if not fraudulent, the mere surface of historical event. 'The thought of nations, like that of individuals,' he writes, 'if it appears perfectly and fully in the inner world of the imagination, never succeeds in revealing itself completely in the world of external reality, thanks to the multitude of disturbing accidents which, entwined like a net across its path, entangle and hold it back, turn it aside, and almost never allow it to go on to its end.'[10]

The only access to a nation's 'inner world of imagination' is that afforded by its artistic creations and, very especially, by its literary works. Literature is the probe that measures the depth of a culture's

affective stratum, as philosophy measures the depth of the intellectual
stratum. This opinion of Giner's is unquestionably of Germanic origin.
Giner has received from Herder and his followers, as a basic idea, the
notion of the existence of a national *genius*, a combination of traits that
give special and unmistakable form to a country's psyche. At first
glance this individuality seems to contradict the principle of universal
harmony which is the mainstay of Krause's doctrine. But in fact there
is no contradiction. When Krause advocates universal harmony, he
does not propose to base it on universal uniformity. And he is absolutely
right about this. Uniformity is possible only at the cost of brutally
cutting off everything that is 'genius-like' – that is, spontaneous and
distinctive – in the individual or race. Uniformity leads unavoidably to
mediocrity. The Krausist idea of harmony is a result, let us repeat, of
the fusion 'of multiplicity in unity, without destroying that multiplicity;
as if, in the cohesion represented by the whole, each part were to
acquire a higher level of existence and knowledge'. Hence nothing must
restrain the full and free expression of national genius; on the contrary,
it must be aided and protected by all possible means. In works of the
imagination, a nation will be all the greater the more faithfully it
exposes the elements that make up its particular character.[11] The same
can be said of literary or artistic creation as of the individual from
whom it proceeds: that it is universal only in the measure in which it is
profoundly human, and profoundly human only in the measure that it
is radically original, for the only thing that is original in man is
precisely that which he shares universally with his fellow men: their
common humanity. Homer, Leonardo da Vinci, Cervantes, Shakespeare, Beethoven, are universal precisely because they are original in
the highest degree, magnificent and induplicable human beings.
'A nation's originality', Giner emphasizes, 'is determined...by two
essential elements, namely: the continuation of tradition at every
moment of its history, and firmness in maintaining the vocation which
inspires that nation and makes it effective in the structure of human
society',[12] or, in other words, to be what it is and to persist in being it,
at all times and under all circumstances of national life.

Now, according to the writer of the essay, 'in France there is no
national originality, nor is it possible that there can be'.[13] To begin with,
in France the medieval tradition lacks vigor, and in other countries
– Spain, for example – it is precisely from that tradition that the
consciousness of historical personality springs. Because of the feebleness
of the tradition in France, French writers have not hesitated to disdain

it, and in the end have rejected it in favor of a literary canon – the classical model – from which the ingredients of a truly national, distinctive, characteristic, concrete literature are excluded. Acceptance of the classical rule has not been entirely due to whim or chance. At all times the Frenchman has displayed:

a certain predilection for what is cultivated, external, and elegant in preference to what is energetic, internal, and powerful; but ever since the time of Francis I, precisely at the most propitious moment for the formation of a national literature, that predilection becomes more and more marked, and with the final triumph of the classical ideal in the seventeenth century...the possibility that France might eventually possess a genuinely national literature vanished forever.[14]

Insubstantiality, versatility, refinement: these seem to be the results of the lack of originality observable in French literature. The chief characteristic of the French genius is that of expressing exquisitely things that everyone knows. A commonplace becomes a literary gem. But it also has another characteristic worthy of mention, namely that of reducing to a finely tooled cliché whatever is profound and complex in the thought of other nations. It might be said that French literature, weary of the monotony and insipidity of its domestic diet, takes over the literary victuals of other countries by the expeditious procedure of steeping them in a French sauce.

The French, who fall in love with the most widely differing things one after another, passing rapidly from one extreme to the other – exception made of a few glorious individuals – in general lack a literature with a stamp of its own, for they depend on that of all the other countries...; only French literature [among ancient and modern literatures] is not deterdetermined by any special quality, and its chief characteristic is to have none and admirably reflect all others.[15]

4. Classicism and romanticism

It must not be forgotten that Giner's study dates from a period in which, in Spain as elsewhere, there was still living memory of the struggle between classicists and romanticists.[16] And it is not strange that he reserves his harshest criticisms for the former, simply because they were the ones who carried the imitation of French models to extremes of degrading servility. In this regard, he reminds his readers that 'that pedantic and bastardized classicism', fruit of 'an artificial and violent culture', was French; French too were 'that dead poetry' and that 'drawing-room literature which evoked ideals that have been lost forever'; French was that reactionary impulse which, with its predilection for the past, forgot 'the later great evolutions of European society'; French was 'that false *bon goût*' and French 'that ridiculous and superficial criticism which applied itself first and foremost to external details'.[17] But indeed, the romanticists receive no kinder treatment. In this regard we must remember that Giner identifies romanticism with French romanticism, perhaps because what was understood as romanticism in Spain was a faithful copy of French models. The writer praises the attempts at rebellion by classicism's enemies, proliferation of literary genres, return to nature, enthusiasm for the real, open expression of sentiment and imagination. But as for romantic enthusiasm for the Middle Ages, Giner says, like a good Krausist, that any attempt to return to the past, in search either of models for imitation or simple inspiration, attacks the very root of art and violates the fundamental laws that rule the human spirit's development. His attitude leaves no room for doubt. It is essential to repudiate outright the inclination toward the medieval in contemporary romanticism – a projection into time of escape from reality, as exoticism is its projection into space. The arguments he employs bear a considerable resemblance to those used by Heine against August Wilhelm Schlegel and his followers, when they are not taken directly – diatribes apart – from *Die romantische Schule*. There is a need, however, to re-evaluate the Middle Ages, disdained by literary rulemakers and art historians as a barbaric parenthesis between two periods of splendour in the West's cultural history. The medieval period must be considered as 'a confused whirlwind, as an immense laboratory where the fusion of the classical world and the Christian world took place', a fusion which is the distinctive feature of the European spirit. But 'to think of the Middle Ages as an *immediately* unifying and concrete determination of humanity...to try to find expressed with systematic clarity in the form of that magnificent period the peculiar elements of that moment of transition and anarchy, of contradiction and struggle, of ferment and tumult...[is] to condemn the world, for reactionary reasons, to the convulsions of a perpetual revolution...to make of the past a model for a mutilated present and an impossible idea for the future'.[18]

In conclusion, according to Giner, romanticism is a reactionary movement. By nostalgically evoking the Middle Ages, in which it tries to see a sort of Paradise Lost, it becomes liable to a perversion not unlike that of its adversary, classicism, which in its turn sighs for a Graeco-Latin antiquity as an embodiment of the Golden Age. Both are false

versions – that is, *perversions* – of historical reality, and they might have
been pardonable as creations of imaginative license if they did not
harbour the malign purpose of degrading modern man and his cultural
creations. Worse still, literary men and artists have used them to escape
the duty – incumbent on them as men – of attending to the needs of
the moment in which they are fated to live. Even in imaginative works,
historical evasion implies irresponsibility, lack of faith, and frequently
even cowardice. Beneath the serene countenance of classicism and the
convulsive face of romanticism, the dispassionate critic can often glimpse
evasive and pusillanimous spirits. It is this desire for escape which is
Giner's chief criticism of romanticism; and the harshness of the re-
proach remains even after the essayist admits that, when it first
appeared, the romantic rebellion was indispensable in order to rescue
art and literature from the sterility to which the devitalized neoclassic
formula had condemned them. What Giner does not do is emphasize
that the escape into medievalism is a characteristic trait of the German
romantic school; and therefore, when he attributes this lamentable
tendency to the 'stupid exclusivism' of French writers, he commits a
serious injustice and in addition reveals the extent of his Gallophobia.
France is guilty, according to him, not only of distorting historical truth
to satisfy an aesthetic whim, but also of confusing the noble principle of
freedom of art with the detestable one of artistic anarchy. Contemporary libertinism – remember that the essay was written in 1862 – has
sanctioned all kinds of excesses which try to dignify themselves by
assuming labels like sentimentalism, realism, or individualism. It would
be unjust, of course, to say that France is the sole source of such perversions. They have existed, and still exist, everywhere. But 'France',
writes Giner, 'has always had a book with blank pages where the first
comer has been able to write his ravings, and a large body of opinion in
every social sphere ready to raise those ravings to the level of a doctrine
and, what is much worse, to make them into institutions...; it fell to
French literature, after all, to adopt the individual aberrations of other
countries.'[19]

7

Krausism and literature

1. The literature of the rising bourgeoisie

It would be useless to try to establish a causal relationship between Krausist doctrine and Spanish literature during the period when that doctrine attained its greatest influence. But, if not so much for the ideas it disseminated as for the spiritual climate it evoked, Krausism brought about perceptible changes in the way of 'making' literature, in the meaning attributed to literary creation, and in the manner of understanding criticism. This 'atmospheric' influence of the imported philosophy was inevitable. It must be remembered that Krausism irrupted into Spanish life at a time when, as a sort of compensation for the weakness shown by other manifestations of the spirit, literature was being intensely cultivated. Such a hypertrophy simply meant that every man with pretensions to intelligence believed himself called, in greater or lesser measure, to try his luck in the field of letters. In nineteenth-century Spain, literature, along with journalism and politics, was one of the ways which the person with no special talents considered most practicable for clambering to fame. Naturally this increase in volume did not bring with it a qualitative increase in literary production, but exactly the opposite. In the years between 1845 and 1874 Spanish letters yielded repeated harvests of mediocrity, with the exception of a few respectable names and one outstanding genius, Bécquer. It was a literature very much in harmony with the tawdry society that produced it. And until that society was shaken up by a summons to some militant ideal, it would continue to produce and enjoy comedies like those of Bretón de los Herreros and Tamayo, novels like those of Fernán Caballero, and poetry like that of Selgas or Campoamor.

However, it is somewhat paradoxical that during the very period when modern Spain was beginning to develop, when the ways of thinking and feeling that were to differentiate modern from traditional Spain were beginning to take shape, the kind of literature produced was trivial, superficial, and short-sighted. It was a combination of meaning-less rhetoric, cloying sentimentality, café-table philosophy, and local-color anecdote. With very few exceptions, the literary men of that twenty-year period tried not to abandon the ideals that had come into vogue with romanticism but to domesticate them, for only in this way could they be adopted by a prudish, colorless, and mercenary society. What finally emerged from this attempt at domestication was sometimes grotesque, often counter-productive, and almost always in doubtful taste. The titles of some works of the period are revealing in this respect: the *Man of the World* replaced the romantic hero, the *New Don Juan* was a vulgar seducer, people flocked to *The Positive* and were ruled by the canon of *The Percentage*; and the despair and self-disgust of the poets of the preceding period was replaced by the hypocritical skep-ticism of the *dolora*, as the rhymed aphorism used by Campoamor was called. The lack of concern and feeling displayed by this literature is especially apparent in the fact that scarcely any trace of serious contem-porary events can be found in it. And this was true not only of the civil wars, social rebellions, and obvious collapse of historical institutions, but also of the changes worked on the repertory of commonplace ideas by philosophy on the one hand and science on the other, and of the genuine uneasiness that resulted from the collision of those new ideas with traditional religious beliefs.

In short, it was an insubstantial and anecdotal kind of literature, one which evaded man's concern with himself, perhaps because its chief purpose consisted in urging him to behave exactly like everyone else, to dissolve his personality in social anonymity. Exercise of the rising bourgeoisie's virtues demanded, as a necessary condition, peace of body and mind. Hence, in the literature of this early Spanish bourgeois period we can see the dual intention of amusing the reader, that is, freeing him from his worries, and of suggesting that he avoid excitement and dis-order. In writers of the period the first thing we notice is the moral, either expressed or tacit. 'Do not try to be different', they seem to warn the reader; 'true happiness lies in not exceeding bounds, and in wanting to be, and in fact being, just like everyone else.' Wilfulness, passion, even talent, are set bounds beyond which the free expression of personality results in derangement, dissatisfaction, social subversion. Frightened by the still-recent writhings of romanticism, the writer of Isabella II's reign hungers for moderation and thirsts for discipline. But it must be kept in mind that moderation and discipline are not aesthetic but social. Literary creation is not subordinated to an artistic precept but to a social precept. Art is placed at the service of a social class and moralizes in the name of the interests of that class.

2. Life, art, and history

Into this frivolous and irresponsible atmosphere Krausism came to proclaim the principle that 'all life is art',[1] and the consequent need for the artist to devote himself in his work to unifying and endowing with meaning the many and varied facets of his own life. Nor is it superfluous in this regard to point out that the Krausist idea of art starts off, as does its idea of science, from the viewpoint of 'unity in variety'. An objective common to both science and art is that of 'organizing' different and many-faceted aspects of the real, reducing to order and harmony what is, though only in apearance, disorder and antagonism.[2] But while in science the organizing instrument is reason, in art it is imagination. What is called 'aesthetic intuition' or 'poetic sense of life' is that special manner of seeing an object 'in such a way that nothing in it seems useless and all that we see...is combined and conditioned with mutual dependence'.[3]

Now, these organizing instruments of reality, reason and imagination, are basic elements in individual consciousness, and act as its irradiations upon the external world. It is true that a Universal Reason exists; but, as has already been seen when we dealt with Krause's metaphysic, the *Wesen* amounts to a sort of projection to the infinite of the unity which the individual finds in his own consciousness. Only by withdrawing from worldly concerns and by introspection can man aspire to 'organize' his interior realm, a condition previous to any subsequent inquiry about God, the world, or humanity. The rational knowledge of reality is an elaboration of the knowledge that man acquires of himself. The same can be said of imagination, or aesthetic intuition. Its function, too, is that of finding the intimate connection between things, of 'organizing' reality. But instead of doing this by analytical and reflective means, it does so synthetically and impulsively, in an instantaneous and immediate vision, as a magical revelation of the essential unity of all created things. 'Imagination...which performs a sort of second creation, sees that unity formally expressed, without explaining its nature or understanding its causes.'[4]

Every work of art springs from inside man; it is 'an intimate and individual event' which struggles to emerge and, having done so, is translated into universally identifiable and significant forms. Hence the work of art is the result of the artist's subjective vision on the one hand and on the other the generalization of that individual intuition. But art also has a temporal and historical facet, and another spatial and socio-cultural facet. A canvas, a bronze, a poem, incorporate a good measure of the time and milieu in which they are produced, as an 'experience of the imagination'; and these factors – determining factors in a certain sense – aid in the task of characterizing the artistic creation and giving it meaning. The fact that great works of art manage to transcend – and make us forget – their location in space and time does not mean that knowledge of that location may not be necessary for certain purposes. To reject it completely, as a certain aesthetic faction recommends, would mean rejecting the man, the time, and the kind of world that inform every work of art; worse still, it would mean forgetting that art, no matter how sublime, is a human outgrowth, perhaps the most deeply and spontaneously human of man's productions. All life is art, of course; but with still more reason, all art is life.[5]

Hence, when we are in the presence of a work of art we should not be surprised if, after the initial aesthetic impression – that is, our spirit's free response to sensorial beauty – we are eager to know the general context of which that work forms part, the location it claims among the other things that crowd the historic and cultural area to which it belongs. Nor is this a capricious wish; far from it. If every work of art is a unitary vision of sensorial reality formed by the imagination, then nothing but art itself can give us a more direct and complete sense of what lies concealed in the heart of a given time or place, precisely that which we vainly seek in ordinary history. Conversely, knowledge of a period – that is, of the social and historical forces at work in it – can guide us, at least in principle, not only in deciding whether that period can be fertile artistically, but also in determining what forms of art are in harmony with it. For 'there are ages in the history of the human spirit when reality is offered to its eyes all at once and complete, as a whole that is ordered and connected in the plenitude of its relationships'.[6] These are the eminently artistic ages. There are others, however, whose 'unity...does not immediately reveal itself to sensorial contemplation and requires, in order to become known, a process of meditation and efforts of the understanding'.[7] These are the ages in which philosophical or scientific creation rules aesthetic creation. But even within each age, it can be seen that one form of art or another stands out above the rest, or that this or that province of science receives more attention than the others. It would be idle to seek the reasons for such a predilection in mere chance or whim. They must be sought in the nature of the link that connects the spirit of the artist or man of science with the spirit of his time and his surroundings. And this search is not the exclusive province of art history and criticism but of general history, if history is to be something more than the skin-deep chronicle of 'facts' it has traditionally been.

For, as Francisco Giner suggests, 'it is natural that history, considered as the mere narration of things as they happened, cannot enlighten us as to their essential nature'.[8] Much more than the historical 'event', we should care about its cause. Knowledge of the former is often motivated by no more than curiosity about something that is odd, surprising, or picturesque. Conversely, when we inquire into causes we find impulses, motives and aspirations that show the depth and complexity of the human soul. We have to go to great art, not history, to discover the 'touch and real meaning of life'. And this is so for a very simple reason: 'an artistic conception, created without an external and secondary purpose which confines it to a certain space, a conception from which arises man's most individual and characteristic attributes, comes into being in a world left to his own free will, with no other yoke than that of his own wishes'.[9] All of man's other creative activities – philosophy, law, science, industry, etc. – arise in response to demands that come to him from outside, needs imposed by the mere fact of living. Alone among his fellow men, the artist enjoys the privilege of obeying 'an inner need of his soul'. And so it is in the fine arts that the authentic feeling of a period is best reflected. The artistic work is the synthesis in which the opposition represented by the artist and his world is harmonized and transcended. This dialectical interpretation of artistic creations is found, either expressly or tacitly, in all the Krausists who have dealt with problems of aesthetics.[10]

3. Literature and society

Literature occupies a privileged place among the fine arts, for, 'because of the means of expression available to it, the almost universal and paramount influence it exercises, the immense variety of the sphere in which it moves, it offers with greater clarity and precision that happy harmony of the general with the individual which is the *summum* of sensorial representation'.[11] But, apart from the intrinsic meaning of the beautiful in literature as a synthesis of the particular and the universal, we must stress the Krausists' enthusiasm for literature and contrast it with the disdain they show for history. History – and in this case they refer only to political history – is 'a mute hulk made of events, a skeleton neither clothed in virile muscle nor quickened by the blood's life-giving heat'.[12] It is useless to ask history what the Athenian of Pericles' time, or the Spaniard of Philip III's, was like. History will give us detailed information about everything but that. The image that history will give us of those periods lacks only one thing: life. And it is precisely life that we capture instantly in a drama by Sophocles or a comedy by Lope. 'Hence, literature is nothing other than the first and firmest way to understand past history.'[13]

And also, of course, to understand contemporary history. In their search for 'life' as a supplement to the incomplete data furnished by mere observation, the Spanish Krausists turn to contemporary literature. At first glance they seem to be guided by the attempt to find symptoms that will permit them to diagnose the temper of the period in which they are fated to live. For there is no doubt that it is the period they know least about. They have fashioned a philosophical and historical perspective of the past in which there is evidence of the progressive realization of an ideal common to humanity as a whole. Of the future they know that sooner or later there will be full achievement of all the promises implicit in the past. But what can be said of the present moment? In reality, very little. Is it perhaps the end of the period of promises? Is it the beginning of the period of fulfillment? There lies the Krausists' anguish, the tragic indecision that can be observed in them when they descend from the impersonal plane of ideas to that of daily concerns and tasks. At what stage are they in their long pilgrimage toward the golden ideal? Krause's imperturbable optimism led him to believe that the stages of groping and preparation had definitely passed. Sanz del Río did not think that the period of bliss had arrived, but he 'felt its presence' through an irresistible inclination of his spirit. His disciples, on the other hand, saw around them nothing but confusion, discouragement, and cynicism. Though without daring to confess it, they could not fail to think that all men, and especially Western man, seemed to be farther away from the hoped-for ideal during the last third of the nineteenth century than in 1811, when Krause wrote his *Urbild der Menschheit*.

And so, what did the Krausists learn from an examination of contemporary letters? Indeed, it could hardly have been more disheartening. On the one hand they discovered a 'physiologism' that harboured the most violent and destructive passions, inconceivable at a time when there was an urgent need to build a just and rational social structure; on the other, they found a 'realistic naturalism' that was a bad copy of both nature and reality; here, a 'coarse individualism', a mixture of egomania and poverty of spirit; there, a 'stylistic virtuosity' to which all ethical aspirations were willingly sacrificed. The literary artist poured into his creations the 'unpleasant disharmony' from which the society of his time was suffering. Stridency, lack of moderation, vulgarity, selfishness, in short all the signs of a world that seemed in process of dissolution, appeared in the literature of the time.[14] 'The spectacle of contemporary letters,' wrote Giner in 1863, 'taken as a whole, is not the one most likely to soothe those who do not feel overwhelming faith in the destiny and survival of art.'[15] But that faith is a side effect, derived from faith in the destiny and survival of the most sublime human creations. Only a person with an unbreakable faith in man and his affairs could overcome the initial disillusionment caused by modern literature. Only literature? No, current art, philosophy, religion, law, and science in general. The error, a very human one, lies in believing to be permanent what is only a transitory phase, a momentary detour among the many revealed by man's historical trajectory. The present is a period of crisis, 'and not an ordinary crisis, limited to this or that particular society on the globe, to this or that element of human life, but universal and including all of them'. And how does this crisis affect the man of the moment? As an anguished vacillation 'between a past that is no longer sufficient and a future that impels him mysteriously, but of whose secret he is still ignorant'.[16] In short, as a desire to escape from the here and now. This desire for escape can be seen in easily identifiable movements like neoclassicism, romanticism, exoticism, occultism, or in others that are less obvious but equally revealing for anyone who takes the trouble to analyze them: the literature of 'the typical', aestheticism, naturalism. Preoccupation with minutiae, with local color, the picturesque detail, or stylistic over-refinement is often only a subterfuge. Amazed by the contradictions around him, incapable of seeing clearly in the tumult of the modern world, the artist seeks refuge in the particular, the diminutive, or the ephemeral. 'Present-day art is the art of vulgarity. Drama has fallen to the level of witty conversation; opera, to an amusing spectacle; lyric poetry, to a ladies' album; painting to the figurine and the antique shop; all of it, in short, to futile pastime, mere secondary ornament of other, more pressing needs.'[17] Did this mean that art, as Hegel had prophesied, had already played its role and must give place to higher concerns?

4. Contemporary lyric poetry

Certainly not. The Krausists believed that only a person who reads history as a series of gradations, and not as a cycle of cycles, could accept so arrogant a statement. The contemporary confusion is characteristic of a period of transition in which, between an unsatisfactory past and an unrevealed future, the artist feels helpless in the midst of an unstable present, with no more resources than those he can draw upon from his own weakness. Left to his own devices, he eventually convinces himself that, once the nexus between imagination and external reality has been broken, the truly essential and permanent reality is that of his own consciousness. There within all is concord, reconciliation, harmony. The outside world is, if not suppressed, at least enclosed in parenthèses, like something subordinate and incidental. But it will be said, and rightly, that there is no possible art without an object, for every work of art is a synthesis of the artist and his world. How can the artist dispense with external reality, with the objective world? Very easily: by objectivizing himself or, which is almost the same thing, partially de-subjectivizing himself, breaking the unity of his own consciousness, so that in the resulting schism one part represents the subject and another the object. In this way 'the imagination at last finds its complement and takes pleasure in the consciousness of its free dominion over a world inaccesible to anyone else, and which belongs only to that imagination'.[18]

The objectivization of the self is the substance of lyricism, and the disturbed present-day period is, in the Krausists' opinion, one in which lyric poetry predominates. 'Why appeal to the external, vainly seeking guidance and light for his inspirations, if he – the poet seems to tell himself – possesses an inexhaustible treasure of harmonies? Such is the question that the spirit asks itself in periods like our own; and to that question...lyric poetry responds.'[19] Hermenegildo Giner calls lyric poetry the poetry of 'variety', as epic poetry is that of 'unity' and dramatic poetry that of 'harmony';[20] and the lyric genre is poetry of variety not only because its object is composed of the innumerable affective states and multiple impressions that the poet discovers within himself, but also because of the extraordinary richness of form into which such poetry is cast. The despotic lyricism of the present period – and let us not forget that the Krausists are speaking of the nineteenth century – has not been satisfied with relegating epic and dramatic poetry to a secondary plane, but has also made them serve ends that are, if not exclusively, at least primarily lyrical. As for the epic, which is or should be the objective poetry *par excellence*, it is useless to seek it in current literature. Neither *Don Juan* nor *Eugene Onegin* nor *La Légende des siècles* nor *El diablo mundo* are unitary representations of sensorial reality, but 'effusions of the heart and dreams of the imagination'. And if, on the other hand, we turn to *Faust* or *Manfred*, so far from finding that inextricable mingling of imagination and the external world which is the essence of dramatic poetry, we discern only splendid creations of the lyric genius.

It is not hard to see that the aestheticians of Krausism interpret the preponderance of the lyric as proof of the imbalance that afflicts contemporary life. For after all, lyricism is an artistic projection of egotism, and this is the shoal on which every attempt at social integration founders:

If each man feels arising in the depths of his being the continual protest of his exclusive ideal against his contemporaries and bends all his efforts on not becoming confused with the rest, on refusing to recognize any supremacy, on breaking every external yoke and on obeying only his personal insirations, lyric poetry has songs for the most conflicting ideals.[21]

Hence the philosophy of history that they profess forces the Krausists to consider as transitory this exclusive predominance of lyricism, destined to wane when the poet, instead of evading the contrarieties of the external world, goes out to meet them and grasps the essential unity that includes them all. But until that time comes it is good to enjoy the creations of present-day lyricism, undoubtedly the most splendid revealed by the history of poetry, and to seek in them 'the immense number of perspectives of reality' into which the image of the contemporary world is fragmented.[22]

5. The novel: a harmonic or polemic genre?

In reality, the reaction against extreme lyricism was much nearer than had been thought, in the years leading up to the September Revolution, by those Krausists who wrote on matters of aesthetics. And moreover, that reaction was about to assume an unexpected form. Despite the wishes of Francisco Giner and Sanz del Río, it did not come about through a revitalization of dramatic poetry – that 'harmonic' poetry so beloved of the Krausists – nor through a return to epic poetry – 'objective' poetry – but through the rapid and protean development of a genre to which the aestheticians of 'harmonism' had paid little attention except to mention it with obvious scorn. This genre was the novel, 'the epic of the century' as Clarín was to call it, repeating a vague definition much in vogue at the time.[23] In 1862 Francisco Giner was still thinking, when he referred to the novel, in terms of *Werther* and *Wilhelm Meister*, of *Notre-Dame de Paris* and *Mauprat*, of *Atala* and *I promessi sposi*, and rightly considered such productions to be lyric poems in prose, if not 'sentimental or pseudo-historical narratives plagued with highly-colored situations, unlifelike characters, unexpected catastrophes'. Absent from these fictions was what Clarín himself called 'artistic altruism'; that is, 'the faculty of applying the imagination, very forcefully and lovingly, to creations which are completely transcendental, which represent different types – in so far as a difference is possible – from that which the author himself could most readily represent'.[24] In other words, the synthesis of individual imagination and external reality – that reality which according to the Krausists was indispensable to any work of art destined to survive in the admiration of men – had not yet taken place. In fact, artistic altruism does not become firmly established until the arrival of Balzac and Flaubert, Gogol and Dickens, creators of the strictly modern novel. In them, and with characteristics that are not important here, epic objectivity combines with lyrical self-concern, with the result that the novel that emerges can aspire, with better credentials than dramatic poetry, to the category of 'harmonic genre' *par excellence*.

In Spain the artistic altruism of which Clarín speaks did not arise until shortly before the Restoration, and its full development was confined to the last quarter of the nineteenth century. Spanish cultivators of the modern novel very soon realized that they had at their disposal an instrument which, owing to its versatility, could be adjusted to any purpose. The Krausist González Serrano writes:

The novel is the literary genre best adapted to the spirit and tendencies of the time we live in. The syncretic nature of the prose poem, the dual nature of its composition, which reveals the artist's personal impressions and judgments as well as the real and objective circumstances accompanying the development of the action; the very broad sphere in which the novelist moves by being able to speak of everything...and lastly, the constant critical spirit that can reign supreme in the novel, are other conditions, each more favorable than the last, which cause that literary genre to have a greater vogue than any of the others.[25]

The fact that the modern novel appears in a period when serious political, religious, and social questions were being aired in Spain, when every man of sensitivity and intelligence felt stirred by very serious misgivings, contributed in large measure to giving the genre a markedly political slant which often made its artistic quality suffer. During the eighteen-seventies, and very especially in the second half of the decade, Galdós, Pereda, and Alarcón did not hesitate to use the novel as a battering ram with which to breach their adversaries' entrenched ideological positions. This was the 'critical spirit' to which González Serrano alludes when he speaks of *Doña Perfecta*. It could be said that when the literary artist, after the extreme lyricism of the previous generation, looks again at the reality around him, he not merely affirms it but affirms it as a source of antagonism. In these early creations of the modern Spanish novel the novelist's 'world' is almost always an ideological antagonist, to be lived with in constant vigilance if not open conflict. Galdós's 'world' in *Doña Perfecta* is religious intolerance, as Pereda's 'world' in *Don Gonzalo González de la Gonzalera* is democracy and that of Alarcón in *El escándalo* lack of religious belief. Here we encounter another symptom of the unmistakable *ideocratic* atmosphere brought into being by the Spanish evolution of Krausism. The view of the external world as a structure of hostile ideas inevitably leads the individual to affirm his own ideology in an absolute and exclusive way; that is, it leads him to exhibit the same intolerance that afflicts his adversary. Let us recall once again the case of León Roch, a fictional Krausist, who when he has to confront hostile reality goes from tolerance to fanaticism, from being the master of his ideas to being their slave. For ideas, it need hardly be said, are dissociative agents, and only by shunning them can men find each other and fraternize on the ground of their common humanity.

And so it is the despotism of ideas that lends the Spanish novel of the eighteen-seventies its polemical character, as it also lends a polemical character to religion, to politics, in short, to all Spanish activities during that decade. That is why the description of 'realistic' commonly applied to this way of understanding fiction does not seem very adequate. Indeed, when examined more closely it seems quite the opposite, at least in intention: it is an 'idealistic' novel, nourished by the desire that things should be different from the way they are, which is the utopian aspiration of all periods troubled by ideocratic passions. Only after 1880, when the intellectual ferment produced by Krausism had abated a little, could a 'realistic' novel properly be spoken of; that is, a novel rooted in a reality not previously reduced to an ideological scheme. But even this phase was a fleeting one. The so-called 'Generation of 1898' would again make the novel into a form of lyric.

6. Literary criticism

Nothing is more effective than criticism in helping to correct the deficiencies and errors of current literature. But in order to do so – and this is the Krausist viewpoint – criticism must begin by correcting its own defects in the light of modern demands which make the task of the responsible critic more difficult, though they also ennoble it.[26] For it must be pointed out that criticism is the exercise of a very serious responsibility which, for that very reason, requires unusual qualities of intellectual and emotional commitment, impartiality, and good sense. In addition to analyzing and evaluating the work of art, the critic also has the delicate duty of uncovering and explaining the historical reality that lives within the artistic creation; for, as has been stated above, it is in art and more particularly in literary art that 'the touch and real meaning of life' are most fully shown. This relevant role played by literature was the reason why several well-known Krausists – Francisco and Hermenegildo Giner, Canalejas, Fernández y González, Federico de Castro, González Serrano – turned enthusiastically to literary criticism, and why several of them made it the object of interesting speculations.

The Krausists find two equally reprehensible attitudes in contemporary criticism. The first of these is radically empirical: 'This is the way it was done in the old days.' The second is radically arbitrary: 'There is no point in arguing about taste.' At one extreme strict tradition raises its banner to repeat its scorn for the present in praises of 'the good old days'. At the other extreme anarchy reigns, aspiring to abolish all standards and to make something that may be a mere presumption on the critic's part pass for true art.[27] Transplanted to the level of criticism, we see the same desire to escape the present that appears in the literature and fine arts of the period. The critic, like the artist, tries to evade the obligations imposed on him by life, unwilling to recognize that living always means 'living in the present', no matter how open the senses may be to any sign that will reveal life's future direction. The literary critic's duty does not consist in pointing out whether this or that composition fits or does not fit into the structure of canons imposed by this or that set of rules. The rules are anachronistic almost by definition. All of them originate to justify *ex post facto* a collection of practices, and to assure with arrogant presumptuousness that those practices have an indefinite life span. Nor does the critic's duty lie in proclaiming that artistic genius is *a-normal* – that is, that it does not recognize norms – and that each work creates its own set of special and untransferable rules, in relation to which it must be analyzed and judged. In this second case there is really no use in talking about criticism, for it would be limited to a sort of trivial casuistry. And so, what role can be assigned to the critic?

To begin with the critic must keep in mind that 'in humanity's historical progression there are always two factors: one is identical, invariable, constant in the unity of its nature; the other is changeable, characteristic, fleeting. Hence, the ideal of a period can also be broken down into two classes of ideals and feelings: accidental and stable, variable and permanent.'[28] It is not, however, a question of two strata with no communication between them. The stratum of the stable, though it is not always the same, 'gradually assimilates those elements that time consolidates so that they will never be destroyed'. The past lives under the surface of the present; better still, it is the authentic present, formed out of the fusion of everything that deserved to survive – that is, to be perpetuated – in all the presents that once were. In consequence yesterday should not be contrasted with today, but rather that which is of all times should be related to that which is of the present. Eternity and temporality are the obverse and reverse of every great work of art. 'Wherever the spirit finds both terms fused into one, it merges with the contemplated work and experiences the pure bliss of the beautiful; wherever one term is lacking, art cannot hope for more than an ephemeral existence which will be swept away with the last vestiges of the fashions to which it has pandered.'[29]

If criticism wishes to be more than the frivolous and often ignoble pastime of the hack journalist or the empty formalism of the rule-maker, it will have to familiarize itself with the progress achieved in a discipline which, in its modern sense, dates from the work of Baumgarten in the middle of the eighteenth century: aesthetics. Harmonic rationalism develops a highly metaphysical idea of aesthetics. It is the duty of aesthetics to bring to light 'absolute philosophical deductions, born from the real study of the eternal laws of the beautiful and of art'. It is the business of criticism to 'distinguish what belongs to that permanent element, from what is subject to perpetual change'.[30] The nineteenth century demands an authoritative, not an authoritarian, criticism; that is, a rational, constructive criticism which will spur the critic to supreme efforts. On this more than on anything else, the Krausists believed, depended the future emergence of a great literature.

8

Krausism and religión

1. The *Syllabus*

In December, 1864, Catholic bishops received a list of eighty propositions entitled *Syllabus complectens praecipuos nostrae aetatis errores*.[1]
The list was accompanied by a letter written on 8 December by
Giacomo Cardinal Antonelli, Pope Pius IX's Secretary of State. On
that same date the pontiff promulgated the encyclical *Quanta cura*,
which can be considered as a declaration of the general principles
demanding censure of some of the propositions enumerated in the
Syllabus. It should be pointed out that the only claim to legality
possessed by the *Syllabus* came from the Secretary of State's letter.
But there is a plausible explanation for this. Each of the errors cited in
the list had been condemned previously in some address, encyclical, or
apostolic letter of Pius IX himself; and so when he ordered them
collected in the form of a catalogue the pontiff undoubtedly decided
that there was no need to set his seal on the condemnation again.
The chief errors to which the *Syllabus* refers are: freethinking, agnosti-
cism, materialism, nationalism, anticlericalism, regalism, liberalism, and
freemasonry.[2]

Publication of the *Syllabus* and the encyclical *Quanta cura* gave rise
to long and bitter polemics, to serious disruptions in the Holy See's
relations with the governments of a number of countries, and in two
cases – those of Austria and Russia – to the abrogation of existing
concordats. Disputes spread to the triple area – theological, political,
and cultural – included directly or indirectly in the pontiff's pronounce-
ments. The favorite subjects for debate were: (a) the value that should
be attributed to a list which had not been expressly made official by the
pope, who had, on the other hand, previously condemned the errors
contained in it; (b) the steps that governments ought to take in view of
the papacy's demands and claims; and (c) the possible effect of the
Syllabus on the cultural life of the Catholic world. Six years of

controversy had scarcely cooled the disputants' vehemence when the definition of the dogma of infallibility added new fuel to the fires of passion. However, it must be pointed out that debates over the dogma of infallibility were primarily of a theological kind, while those that swirled around the *Syllabus* presented, more than anything else, a political and intellectual character. The *Syllabus* pertained directly and immediately to the conduct of the individual Catholic considered in his historical circumstance. But the doctrine of infallibility was more of a theological problem, and although no one was unaware of its possible political consequences, it was theologians and church historians who applied themselves most enthusiastically to the task of explaining it, commenting upon it, or attacking it.

In Catholic countries there were some who interpreted the encyclical and the *Syllabus* as indications of an attempt, considered praiseworthy by many, if not to recover for the Holy See the primacy over the secular arm which it had enjoyed in ancient times, at least to counteract the growing arrogance of civil government; but others believed that the papacy's aims were anachronistic and should be treated as survivals of ecclesiastic medievalism, one more proof of Catholic obscurantism. Some commentators argued that the pope had merely claimed what had always been recognized as the Church's right; namely, full power in questions of doctrine, morals, and internal government; to this others objected that the Church included the individual's entire life under the title of 'morals', and that what the pope was really trying to do was to submit every one of a Catholic's actions to review by ecclesiastical authorities. Nor was there a lack of persons who saw in the Holy See's new attitude a sign that difficult times were coming, times when the Church, in order to triumph over its numerous enemies, would have to present itself to them as a rigidly disciplined army ready to bear any sort of hardships. And lastly, there were not a few who accused the papacy of having finally embraced the doctrine – dear to the Jesuits – of absolute ecclesiastical centralization, and of attempting the destruction of episcopal autonomy in order to put this into practice, thereby forcing the bishops to refer any matter of a certain importance to the Roman Curia. Those who believed this thought they saw conclusive proof of it in the definition of the dogma of papal infallibility.[3]

In Spain, the bishops began publication of the pontifical documents in the early days of 1865. It soon became apparent that direct communication to the episcopate of a declaration through which the pope specifically exempted the Church from all dependence on civil authority, and which held in addition that prelates must publish apostolic decisions without previously consulting that authority, was destined to arouse very rebellious feelings. Tempers soon began to flare. Enemies of the *Syllabus* applauded as an example worthy of imitation the way in which France had responded to the challenge offered by Pius IX. The reactionary government of Napoleon III had banned publication of almost the entire document and summarily suspended publication of *L'Univers*, the only newspaper that had dared to print the document in its entirety. In Spain, as was to be expected, things did not go so far, though there was no lack of serious complications. Liberal newspapers offered abundant examples of the repugnance with which they viewed the papacy's claims, judging them more appropriate to the times of Gregory VII than to those of Pius IX. The government itself, at the time in the moderate party's hands, felt obliged to defend the Crown's prerogatives and consequently to disapprove the procedure used in publication of the papal documents. The Pragmatic Sanction of 1768 was still in force, prohibiting circulation of bulls, rescripts, and apostolic letters that did not bear the Council of Castile's approval. The Minister of Justice used this pragmatic as an excuse when he requested, on 17 January 1865, that the Council of State decide on withholding or release of the encyclical and *Syllabus*. The Council was unanimous in deploring the fact that the Holy See had not announced its intentions to the secular authority before proceeding to publication of both papal declarations. A majority of the councillors expressed themselves in favour of withholding four propositions that were particularly offensive to the rights and prerogatives of the civil power, and recommended release of the remaining seventy-six; they also requested that Article 145 of the Penal Code be applied to the bishops, and that the Nuncio be admonished for having transmitted the documents directly to the episcopate in contravention of the Pragmatic of 1768. But in the end the majority opinion was ignored. On 7 March 1865 the official *Gaceta* published the Spanish version of the entire text of the encyclical and the *Syllabus*. The moderate government confined itself to announcing that it would enforce fully the Pragmatic of 1768 and all laws having to do with the circulation of apostolic documents.[4]

2. Liberal Catholicism

On 18 August 1863, sixteen months before promulgation of the *Syllabus*, the opening ceremonies of a general assembly of Catholics were held in Malines, seat of the metropolitan archbishopric of Belgium. A group of clerics and laymen numbering some 2500 persons met there, along with important representatives of the high ecclesiastical hierarchy. The cardinal-archbishop of Malines headed a delegation of Belgian prelates among whom were the bishops of Namur, Tournai, and Ghent. Cardinal Wiseman, archbishop of Westminster, attended at the head of a group of English bishops. The Nuncio was also present, as was the bishop of Jerusalem. The presiding officer of the Congress was Baron Étienne de Gerlache, perhaps the most notable figure in the Belgian Catholic party.[5]

And yet the most remarkable feature of this assembly, the first of its kind, was not the presence of so many dignitaries of the Church. Clerics and laymen had gathered in Malines to hear the most eloquent champion of *liberal Catholicism.* Count Charles de Montalembert, a former collaborator of Lacordaire and Lammenais and founder along with them of the newspaper *L'Avenir.* Lammenais had died in 1854 and Lacordaire in 1861, and Montalembert continued almost single-handed the campaign in favor of *the free Church in the free State* against the ultramontane faction, headed by Louis Veuillot, editor of the newspaper *L'Univers,* and against the freethinkers who wrote for *Revue des Deux Mondes.* However, for more than ten years the famous Catholic writer had wielded his pen with a caution that had given rise to all sorts of conjectures, a further reason why his participation in the Congress of Malines aroused the liveliest curiosity.

The public session of 21 August was given over to Montalembert's first speech. From the opening paragraphs it became apparent that (a) the speaker had the approval of the immense majority of the audience; and (b) that almost the only ones who listened to him with suspicion or open displeasure were representatives of the higher clergy. Montalembert took pains to show that the Catholic Church's claim to be recognized and protected by the State to the exclusion of any other religious confession was, at this stage in history, completely inadmissible. In his opinion the ultramontane party's theocratic ambitions, viewed from a nineteenth-century perspective, were not only utopian but counter-productive, fated as they were to attract inevitably the ill-will of impassioned democrats toward the Church. 'Many [Catholics]', said the speaker, 'still belong in heart, in spirit, and without fully realizing it, to the *ancien régime*; that is, to the regime that did not permit civil equality or political freedom or freedom of conscience. This *ancien régime* had a great and splendid side. I do not intend to judge it here, and still less to condemn it. I shall merely point out a defect in it, a very important one: it is dead and will never rise again anywhere.' The speaker, convinced that the Church had never suffered so much hardship and unpleasantness as when it had been protected by secular authority, went on to illustrate his thesis by contrasting the condition of the French Church while the Edict of Nantes was in force with its condition after revocation of the Edict in 1685. When it was promulgated in 1598 'there was an immediate and magnificent flowering of Catholic genius, discipline, eloquence, piety, and charity which places the seventeenth century in the first rank of all the centuries of the Church'. Once the Edict was revoked, 'everyone saw in it the triumph of the Church. Orthodoxy was thought to be assured and heresy rooted out forever. But what happened was the exact opposite...Revocation of the Edict of Nantes was not only the signal for an odious persecution, but the hypocrisies and inhumanities that accompanied it were one of the chief causes for the laxity of the clergy, for the calamities and profanations of the eighteenth century.' The speaker believed that it was very important for the Church to accept the principles and usages of modern society and to extract from them, without resorting to deceit or trickery, the greatest possible advantage. Such a procedure 'would be a thousand times less humiliating than having to obtain everything, now from a prince, which is the clumsiest of decoys, now from the reconstruction of an aristocracy, which is the most chimerical of utopias'. Those who called for an unbreakable alliance of Church and State forgot that, as a logical result of such a coalition, the Church would be obliged to share her ally's fortunes: 'If a new Revolution were to break out today,' said the speaker, 'we would tremble to think of the ransom the clergy would have to pay for the illusory solidarity which has seemed to exist for many years between the Church and the [Second] Empire.'

Montalembert's second speech had to do with freedom of worship, and like the previous one it attracted a large audience. In view of the publicity given to the subject of this second speech, it was not strange that some of the dignitaries who had been present at the public session of 21 August abstained from attending on the following day. Their absence caused a certain uneasiness, but this did not prevent the audience from approving with frequent applause the ideas expressed by the speaker. Montalembert began by confirming Guizot's well-known formula on freedom of worship: 'The principle of religious freedom consists exclusively in admitting the right of the human conscience not to be governed in its relationships with God by human decrees and punishments.' It is therefore necessary to exclude the State from any intervention in religious matters; but at the same time, that exclusion presupposes the impossibility of appealing to civil authority to demand protection against dissidence or error. Freedom, certainly, full freedom, but freedom for all religious confessions, freedom even for error. And to demand it does not imply abdication of all that the Church has upheld from time immemorial, but simply the recognition that history reveals an infinite number of atrocities committed in the name of religious truth. 'The Spanish inquisitor who said to the heretic, "truth or death" is as hateful to me as the French terrorist who said to my grandfather "liberty, fraternity, or death." The human conscience has the right to demand that it never be forced to choose between these horrifying alternatives.'

But the establishment of freedom of worship is inescapable for another reason: the patent decline of the Church in countries where it has had the support of the secular arm. It is illusory to believe that Catholicism can prosper wherever it has succeeded in becoming a part of secular laws. The State's guardianship is asphyxiating. 'Italy, Spain, and Portugal are there to prove the basic impotence of the repressive system, of the old alliance between altar and throne to defend Catholicism. Nowhere else, moreover, has religion received crueler wounds; nowhere have its rights been more neglected. The governments of both peninsulas believed that they had established in them a hermetic blockade of the modern spirit, and nowhere has that spirit made greater inroads.' Montalembert went on to review the effects of clerical despotism in Spain under Ferdinand VII, in the Two Sicilies under Ferdinand II, and in the Piedmont of Charles Albert: 'a general deadening of souls and intelligence among honorable people; an impotent anger among a small number of zealots, and among the rest a fanatical passion for evil. The public spirit had been shackled and suffocated, and roused itself only to go over to the enemy. False liberalism, atheism, hatred for the Church had invaded everything. Those parasites of religious absolutism have become the scandal and despair of all Catholic hearts.'

The situation of Catholicism is very different in those countries where the Church has no more protection than that of common law, and has to deal as well with the presence of other confessions: England, Belgium, the United States. The speaker stressed the Church's remarkable vigor under such circumstances, a vigor that showed itself not only in numerical expansion but in a deepening of religious feeling. Nothing proves better than this that laxity is the result of monopoly. In places where the Church may be attacked, the need to defend herself forces her into constant vigilance and inner discipline. 'Yes, Catholics,' concluded Montalembert, 'let the lesson sink in; if you want freedom for yourselves you must want it for all men and in every clime. If you ask it only for yourselves it will never be vouchsafed you. Give it where you are masters, so that it will be given where you are slaves.'[6]

I have thought it useful to quote verbatim a few significant portions of Montalembert's speeches, for they display the aspirations of so-called 'liberal Catholicism'. To call the declaration of Malines a 'manifesto' would be a patent exaggeration, though certainly an excusable one, since its tone, its revelation of motives and intentions, and the circumstances in which it was spoken make it seem more like a manifesto than anything else. But it must be noted that liberal Catholicism was not a *movement* of ideas held by a group of persons who worked for categorical *reforms*. The very nature of Catholicism is hostile to the organization of groups where there is a desire, stated more or less clearly, to admonish or simply to advise Church authorities. And so Montalembert was expressing strictly personal opinions – opinions shared, it is true, by a large number of his hearers, but only as vague aspirations. The most notable feature of liberal Catholicism was that, despite the nobility of its intentions and the talent of its representative men, it could never rid itself of doubts and fears. The specter of dissidence paralyzed the cowardly and troubled those with stronger spirits. Even in the first Congress of Malines the audience's attention was divided between Montalembert and the effect produced by his words on the ecclesiastical dignitaries who had come to hear him. This uneasiness became still more apparent in the second Congress, also held in Malines in August, 1864, three months before publication of the *Syllabus*. Between the two assemblies there had been a letter from Pius IX to the archbishop of Munich in which the pontiff deplored the convocation of such meetings and insisted that the submission of Catholics to the authority of Christ's vicar on earth must not be confined exclusively to matters of faith. But despite Rome's obvious hostility a third Congress of Malines took place in September, 1867, at which the principal speakers were Monsignor Dupanloup, bishop of Orléans, and the famous Father Hyacinthe Loyson. The propositions of the *Syllabus* floated menacingly above the participants' heads. It was obvious that 'the Congress could not, without betraying its own tenets, support a document that condemned ideas and principles it had previously acclaimed with such burning and sincere enthusiasm. But how to protest without falling into schism? What was there to do? To dissolve, to stop meeting; there was no other solution.' Liberal Catholicism, as understood by Montalembert, had received a mortal wound. The definition of the dogma of infallibility finished it off. Montalembert submitted, and spent the remaining months of his life in almost total silence. Father Hyacinthe rebelled and was excommunicated. 'We are in full clerical reaction,' wrote Molinari in 1875, 'and anyone who dared to speak today as they did at the first Congress of Malines would be considered a schismatic.'

3. The religious 'problem' in Spain

Just at the time to which Molinari refers, the religious 'problem' began to be talked about in Spain with remarkable insistence: 'the most awe-inspiring', said Palacio Valdés about the middle of 1875, 'of all those which affect society at the present time'.[7] The largest role in sketching the shape of this 'problem' was played by the periodical press. With the publicity it gave to the declarations of Pius IX, the excommunication of Döllinger and Father Hyacinthe, the schism of the 'old Catholics', the measures taken by the German cabinet under Falk – the basis for Bismarck's *Kulturkampf* – and so on, the belief began to spread that there was also a religious 'problem' in Spain, on whose satisfactory solution depended social well-being and the future of culture.

Now, it is undeniable that nineteenth-century Spain had inherited a problem created long before by the indigenous version of militant Catholicism. The support which part of the Spanish clergy had given, and still gave, to every aim and practice of absolutism, the clergy's intransigence with regard to any ideological novelty, especially if it came from outside the country, the attacks on intelligence perpetrated by the cabinet minister Orovio in the name of unity of faith, the ultramontane reaction of 1875–1881, etc., all seemed to corroborate the fact that there was a 'problem', and a sizeable problem at that. But it would be incorrect to think of it as a religious problem, for although religion entered in, it did so in spite of itself and rather incidentally. It was the clergy, in their wordly activities, their greed for secular privileges, their tentacle-like gropings into every level of life, their desire to maintain their prerogatives and immunities even at the cost of the public weal, who complicated a situation which, though it had been serious for a long time, was to reverberate throughout the nineteenth century with echoes of crisis. And this difficult situation was made manifest in two conflicts: one was jurisdictional, between ecclesiastical authority and civil power; the other was political and ideological, between the State–Church coalition and the liberal spirit of the period. Regalists and anti-clericals made common cause. The regalists impugned the clergy's aims in the arena of high-level politics; the anticlericals did the same in the area, and with the weapons, of day-to-day politics.

Strictly speaking there was no 'religious problem', for the privileged position occupied in Spain by Catholicism was not disputed by any dissident sect; this, however, did not mean that Catholicism lacked rivals. Menéndez Pelayo is not far from the truth when he says that 'the only religion of non-Catholic Spaniards' was 'brutal indifference'.[8] Méndez Bejarano expresses more or less the same opinion when he declares that 'there is no middle ground in Spain's religious conscious-ness: [it is] either Catholic or atheistic'.[9] The nature of that indifference or atheism is not hard to diagnose. It is, in fact, the exact opposite of that typically Spanish 'blind faith' which Unamuno sometimes tell us about.[10] He writes in 1900:

Here [in Spain] we have suffered from acute dogmatism for a long time; here the immanent, intimate, and social Inquisition has always ruled, the Inquisition of which the historical and national version was merely a passing phenomenon...; every Spaniard is an unconscious Manichean; he believes in a Divinity whose two persons are God and the Devil, absolute affirmation, absolute negation, the origin of good and true ideas and that of bad and false ones.[11]

4 Fernando de Castro and his disciples

But if this is true, it is also true that there was no lack of sincerely religious persons who tried to flee from 'absolute affirmation' without falling into 'absolute negation'; persons seeking an intermediate position between the blind dogmatism of the fanatic and the no less blind dogmatism of the café-table Voltairian. And it is precisely in this handful of men, condemned to isolation by the very unpopularity of their attitude toward religion, that we must examine the real Spanish religious 'problem' of the last century. Note that, if it is to be genuine, every religious 'problem' must bear upon it the mark of a personality; it is a 'problem' precisely because the individual conscience sets it before that conscience as an inexhaustible source of doubts and per-plexities. The outstanding example of a Spaniard who incarnated a religious 'problem', that is, a man who made uncertainty the stuff of his life, is, of course, Unamuno. In him the exteriorization of his inner anguish about religious faith became a fertile subject for thought as well as – in the best of all possible senses – a subject for literature. But though he is the most famous, Unamuno was far from being the first of the anchorites of doubt in modern Spain. Half a century before publication of *Del sentimiento trágico de la vida* there was the well-known case of Fernando de Castro, first a discalced Franciscan and later a secular priest, Isabella II's chaplain and, after the September Revolution, rector of the University of Madrid.[12] His break with the Church, which occurred in 1870, was the subject of harsh polemics and had extremely bitter repercussions. Castro's case, stripped of all the unfortunate publicity which clung to the break, came down to that of 'the sincere and pious thinker who respects all manifestations of the religious spirit, who withdraws from a communion because his conscience absolutely demands it, and who amid all the vicissitudes of his belief keeps alive in his soul the eternal foundations of religion'.[13] It is extremely difficult to doubt Castro's integrity. The struggle within him was a long time maturing, an anguished battle between deep religious feeling and growing aversion to the Catholicism of the day. He was a tormented being whose case dramatized the rebellion of spirit against form in the area of religion. Perhaps for that reason his recalcitrance was misunderstood by those who did not realize that it was substantially identical to other contemporary European attitudes: Loyson, Döllinger, Friedrich, Frohschammer, Huber, etc.

What manner of man was Castro? Francisco Giner has left us a portrait of him which only the most inveterate sectarianism has dared to contradict: 'A reflective spirit, inspired by a lofty moral sense which partakes simultaneously of the stoic's austerity and the Christian's sweetness; manly character, used to combining frankness and openness with common sense and circumspection...uniting in his person the dual ministry of faith and reason, as if he wished to give witness by this very fact to their inner alliance.'[14] That external moderation and plainness, however, concealed a heart lashed by anxieties and torturing doubts. Nothing can better help us to understand the extent of this inner agitation than the confession Castro interpolated into the famous speech he made on his reception into the Academy of History. The paragraph appears to be a spontaneous revelation, one of those declarations that sometimes slip out inopportunely, like sudden flashes that reveal our true preoccupations. The brand-new academician said:

I foresee dangers which, though they do not frighten the man who fears God and rests assured on the approval of his clear conscience – rather, he faces them with his head high and his heart serene – yet will they trouble him in those moments when man is weak and feels his insignificance, because they will make him wonder if perhaps he errs and those who contradict him are right; if it would not perchance be wiser to follow the crowd that goes on broad and spacious roads, though they end in death... or to associate himself with the few who climb upward on narrow paths, though in the long run they end in life; for to end in life is to follow the course of reason and the very narrow path that leads to the temple of truth.[15]

Poor Don Fernando! He had rejected mortification of the flesh for that of the spirit, and to the end of his days he never ceased to ask himself if the shift had been the result of weakness, as he feared, or strength of spirit, as he wanted to believe. His agony, for such painful vacillation merits the name, invites comparisons with Unamuno's, though we soon see that it is of the opposite sign. In Don Miguel faith said yes and reason no; in Don Fernando faith said no and reason yes. Sanz del Río's intimate friend and loyal collaborator, a student of harmonic rationalism, a zealous defender of the Krausist philosophy of history, Castro assumed very early in his career the thorny task performed by such men as Ketteler, Dupanloup, Wiseman, Gratry, etc., all of them important figures in the tolerant and large-spirited branch of nineteenth-century Catholic thought. As the outstanding representative of liberal Catholicism in Spain he was the spokesman, perhaps against his will, for the aspirations of a group of intellectuals who believed that agreement was possible between the Catholic Church and the spirit of the century. It must be remembered that these were the years of indecision that stretched from 1864 to 1870, critical years indeed for a large number of Catholics who had been disturbed by the dilemma in which the *Syllabus* had placed them: Catholicism or modern life. On the other hand, it was unquestionable that no amount of casuistry could soften the impact of the famous Proposition 80, which condemned anyone who upheld the opinion that the pope could or should be reconciled 'with progress, with liberalism, and with recent civilization'.[16] No proposition of the *Syllabus* lent itself to double meanings: the whole document is a model of clear language. And yet, we have already seen that liberal Catholicism did not give up the struggle in France and Belgium until 1867. Hence it is not strange that in 1866 there were still people who cherished hopes of accommodation, though such hopes grew weaker daily. It was Francisco Giner who expressed, in manly and dignified tones, the desires and fears of this group which approved of Fernando de Castro's attitude:

The force of events, though not his own wishes, has placed a banner in his [Castro's] hands; and we who have the honor and good fortune to follow it could not wish to see it unfurled by a more valiant arm...If in fact he wins, at least in his spirit and inclinations, we will salute the dawn of happier times than those we are living in now...were he to be defeated, routed, and jeered at in the struggle – God forbid! – then there would no longer be, in the human sphere, any possible hope of salvation among us for so holy a cause.[17]

Up to 1870 Fernando de Castro's campaign was inspired by a dual aim: (a) that the Spanish Church should recover its historical individuality without losing the submission and obedience it owed to the Roman pontiff; and (b) to persuade the Spanish clergy that they should view the new social and political doctrines sympathetically, for the Church's full freedom was implicit in them. It was, in fact, the doctrine of *the free Church in the free State* that Montalembert had defended, but which was now upheld with redoubled energy, for indications of a line of conduct radically different from that proposed by liberal Catholicism were arriving from Rome. The Vatican Council eventually showed how illusory had been the hopes of those who thought that agreement was possible between political freedom and the Roman Curia.[18] In Spain, as elsewhere, the definition of the dogma of infallibility split liberal Catholics into two groups: one submitted to the pope's authority, the other broke with Rome forever.[19] To this second group belonged most of the Krausists and not a few literary men, politicians, and scientists, who went over to the camp of advanced liberalism.

5. Rational Christianity

And what was the effect of the break with Rome on the chief members of the recusant group? First of all, it launched them on a search for a solution to the religious 'problem' created by that rupture: a search for the only authentic problem, namely their own highly personal and untransferable problem. For, as one of the dissidents remarked:

we have torn orthodoxy out of the bosom of present-day society, and this is an important fact; for in religion as in politics, to break with the traditional means condemning oneself to a painful and turbulent pilgrimage through the genuine labyrinth which our century's feverish activity creates and constantly makes more complex. It is necessary to adopt a resolution, in a manly and noble way, in this spiritual crisis.[20]

And indeed, after 1870 part of the Spanish intellectual group gradually moved toward a form of 'rational Christianity' or 'natural religion'. This manifestation of religion claims to arise from

the present-day insufficiency of all the positive religions which have appeared in history up till now; it recognizes the need for a real link between God and man, declaring that link to be purely natural and rational and rejecting any dogmatic element, any mystery, any revelation, and any miracle. The existence and providence of God and the immortality of the soul are perhaps the only principles common to this whole train of thought, which in France and America displays an essentially sentimental and ethical character and in Germany an essentially intellectual one, where God is only the *Absolute Being*, not the *Living God*, and religion is almost absorbed in metaphysics.[21]

Both the intellectual and the sentimental tendencies found partisans among the Spanish disciples of Krause. To the first group belonged Sanz del Río, Salmerón, and Canalejas; to the second Fernando de Castro (after his break with Rome,) Azcárate, and Francisco Giner. But we may ask: is there some link between natural religion and rational Christianity? Cannot the former exist independently of the latter? In theory, yes; but in practice it is very doubtful. For experience shows that when that humanitarian idealism which is 'natural religion' tries to take stock of itself and 'seeks a name for its God, a law for its activity, and a word of hope for its discouragement, it can only find the dogmas of the Church; nor can it glorify any other ethics than Christian ethics, nor stammer anything but the prayers with which the faithful lift their hearts to Providence'.[22] Therefore, all the Krausists considered themselves Christians at bottom, perhaps because they believed that 'the idea of humanity is undoubtedly a creation of Christianity',[23] and because 'the highest and most divine manifestation of the religious life, until now, is the Christian manifestation'.[24] But we must stress the importance of the words 'until now'. For it must not be forgotten that Christianity, for the Krausist, is merely one stage in the religious evolution of humanity; that it will be superseded some day, and that it will then pass into history as one more signpost marking the painful journey toward what Krause was wont to call 'the coexistence of humanity with God as Supreme Being'. The goal of such an evolution is, as has already been noted, a religion without dogmas or mysteries or miracles or revelations, based on the conviction that reason is sufficient to know God and that 'recognition of God and his absolute properties is the only religion worthy of humanity'.[25]

The only differences among the Spanish Krausists as far as religion was concerned were, after all, quite relative; that is, they arose from the position which each of them assumed in that progress toward the religion of humanity. The 'metaphysicians' of harmonic rationalism, Sanz del Río and Salmerón, were very close to complete identification of religion with metaphysics, of religious feeling with philosophical thought. Canalejas, the historian of positive religions, sought in them what all religions possess of substance and permanence, a sort of basic universal religion, free of 'the molds into which accident and circumstance have cast it'.[26] In short, what he wanted to find was – if the paradox is permissible – a rational faith. And lastly, Fernando de Castro, Azcárate, and Giner were still within Christianity, though they had moved a considerable distance in the direction of natural religion. All three of them followed with profound attention the changes that were taking place in the bosom of the Christian confessions, trying to glimpse in them some foretaste of the new universal order. They saw in the secession of the so-called 'old Catholics'[27] a result of the movement favoring the liberalization of Catholicism and a possible portent of an evolution toward deism. They thought they perceived a similar evolution when they turned their attention to the anti-evangelical and free-thinking branch of Protestantism represented by theologians like Bunsen, Baader, Dorner, Pfleiderer, Schenkel, etc. This led Francisco Giner to state, in 1876, that 'the religious question has entered upon a new phase in civilized nations, when it is no longer a question for sincerely pious souls of deciding between Catholicism and Protestantism, but between natural religion and revealed religion'.[28] A Krausist, therefore, tended to interpret the dissidences that were appearing in the Catholic and Protestant orthodoxies as undeniable proof of a move toward the religious attitude of rationalism, in which spirits divided by exclusivist confessionalism and dogmatic intolerance would eventually become reconciled.

But no one has described better than Azcárate the religious evolution of the individual Krausist. In a little book crammed with autobiographical information[29] he passes in review all the reasons and circumstances that have gradually drawn him away from Catholic orthodoxy and impelled him toward a form of rational Christianity. The religious position he finally reaches is:

the point of conjunction where philosophy and positive religion, rationalist theism and Protestant Christianity, have come together, and which has many adepts in Switzerland, France, and England, and still more in the

North American states, homeland of the famous [William Ellery] Channing and of [Theodore] Parker. Think what you will of this tendency, it always represents obvious progress in comparison with the immediately preceding period, for on the one hand religion is confirmed as an aim which is both formal and substantive, and the substantial value of historical manifestations of the religious life, especially Christian life, is recognized; and on the other, it avoids the narrow dogmatic spirit and opens up old molds of thought to new conceptions, making this sphere of existence partake of the general laws which preside over the development of humanity.[30]

The point of conjunction is a profession of faith very similar to that of Unitarianism. Azcárate sums it up as belief in a personal and provident God, in immortality, in the essential truth of all religions, and in Christianity as the highest manifestation of the religious life. He has good reason to declare that the Christian practice he most admires is that preached by 'the famous Channing, whose works', he adds, 'had contributed in large part to confirming my religious ideas'.[31]

9

Krausism and politics

1. The Restoration: differing opinions

The *coup d'état* of 29 December 1874 had the dual effect of quelling social and political unrest and finishing off most of the intellectual effervescence that had given so individual a stamp to the period immediately preceding and following the September Revolution. The Restoration's avowed intent was to return to normal conditions as soon as possible, to re-establish 'historical continuity', to think and act, in short, as if the six years of revolutionary storms had been merely a nightmare from which the country had awakened shattered, but sure that it would be very unlikely to happen again. In Cánovas the monarchy had found an effective architect for its policies. And in Cánovas too, most Spaniards thought they saw the statesman who best embodied the hopes of the moment. For a long time now nothing had seemed more desirable to the Spaniard than social peace, understood as peace founded on a collective desire for conciliation and not the peace that comes from repressive measures. The fleeting periods of calm that had punctuated the century up till then seemed mere armed truces, parentheses opened by exhaustion in the endless civil strife. Cánovas, a man endowed with great political perspicacity, was aware of the immense reservoir of energies and enthusiasms that would be placed at the monarchy's service if it really worked to satisfy the desire for peace harbored in so many hearts. And indeed, 'order', 'peace', and 'work' were the hypnotic words with which Cánovas tried to still the suspicions aroused in no few persons by the Bourbons' return.

Lately there have been many indications that the harshly negative concept of the Restoration held a few decades ago has gradually softened. An example of extreme acerbity is offered by Ortega y Gasset. In his famous speech on 23 March 1914 in the Teatro de la Comedia in Madrid,[1] Ortega said that the Restoration had been 'organized corruption', and added, 'it was a panorama of phantoms, and Cánovas the great impresario of the phantasmagoric'.[2] It was necessary, he said, to organize a political movement whose *raison d'être* would be the repudiation of the network of fictions of which 'official' Spain consisted. It was of primary importance to banish from public life 'conventionalism', 'simplism', and 'encouragement of incompetence', all distinctive traits of the Restoration according to the speaker. A year before Ortega's speech the writer Azorín, in tracing the portrait of the Generation of 1898, stressed the fact that the group known by this name had arisen as a protest against 'the old'; and what was old was the little Spanish world of the last quarter of the nineteenth century:

the vicious practices of our politics, administrative corruption, incompetence, chicanery, nepotism, political bossism, verborrhea, the 'mañana' syndrome, parliamentary cant, personal attacks under the guise of grandiloquent speeches, the 'political arrangements' that make even the best-inclined persons stray from the path of virtue, falsified election results, the chairmanship and management of large companies placed in the hands of influential board members, the useless interlocking gears of bureaucracy...[3]

Though he stresses social rather than political factors, Fernández Almagro writes in almost identical vein to the two previous writers. During the Restoration and Regency:

an almost infantile irresponsibility ruled Spaniards' impassioned comings and goings, with respect to the questions raised by immediate reality. No one looked far ahead. Irresponsibility and optimism...Completely carefree, people dedicated themselves to their favorite pastimes. They shared the triumphs of bullfighters and opera singers, orators, facile poets, and writers of pleasant prose...What a happy age and what happy years were those![4]

It would be superfluous to add more quotations – from Costa, Maeztu, Fernández Villegas, Unamuno, Baroja, Gómez de Baquero, etc. – which would simply repeat very similar sentiments in different words. After the colonial disaster the intellectuals concentrated upon 'the men of the Restoration' all the responsibility for the misfortunes of the moment.

And yet we are troubled by the suspicion that such opinions have hidden from us a good part of the truth. Who were, in fact, these 'men of the Restoration' and the Regency, stepchild of the Restoration, who are accused of being responsible for the tragic pantomime? Let us find out. In politics their names are Cánovas and Castelar, Sagasta and Salmerón, Moret and Silvela; in literature – reducing the firmament to a single constellation – they are Galdós and Clarín, Valera and Pereda, Echegaray and Pardo Bazán; in philology, in its broadest sense, Menéndez Pelayo; in medicine, Cajal; in pedagogy, Giner; in sociology, Azcárate and Posada; in history of jurisprudence, Hinojosa and Costa. The list could be lengthened at will. Well, do these men deserve the reproaches heaped upon them after 1898? It must be admitted that they do not. Obviously, in the biliousness with which the twentieth century judges the last quarter of the nineteenth there is a good deal of the blind negativism that bubbles in the wake of great crises; those crises which, by shaking up the collective conscience, leave dregs of anger and resentment. Why does the Restoration have to be solely responsible for the defeat of 1898? Why not the whole nineteenth century, and even the eighteenth and the seventeenth? And indeed, in the same speech in which he makes Cánovas responsible for 'the stop-page of national life', Ortega offers a statement that seems to deny his accusation:

What Spain represents, unlike the other present-day peoples of Europe, is a nation where it is not this or that group of men, this or that set of institutions, which have failed but rather something deeper: it is that in our history we have something resembling a breakdown in the effectiveness of the most intimate and inalienable principles of the people, of tradition.[5]

In open disagreement with the opinions we have cited is a more recent one by Gregorio Marañón, included in the essay that serves as a preface to *Vida de Antonio Machado y Manuel*, by Miguel Pérez Ferrero.[6] Dated in April, 1939, this essay reflects the nostalgia with which its author recalls, just after the end of the Spanish Civil War, 'one of the great periods of Spanish genius...which begins with the Restoration and swells like a magnificent wave, reaching its highest point in the Generation of 98 and those other generations that lived in the first third of our century...'[7] The tacit watchword is unmistakable: *Nessun maggior dolore*...Marañón continues, 'The great sorrow of these present days has been necessary to make us realize the good things we have lost, and their magnitude. When we evoke them we feel an inexpressible melancholy.'[8] But in what did the special greatness of that period – a period, according to some, worthy of being considered a second Golden Age – consist? In its *liberalism*, using the word in a much broader sense than it is usually given; namely, integrity, generosity, tolerance, respect. Marañón himself dilates upon the mean-ing of that period and that liberal spirit in another essay written as a prologue to the *Epistolario* of Leopoldo Alas and Menéndez Pelayo.[9]

The period he describes is 'the time of conciliation', and the liberal spirit is 'the humanist attitude'. Marañón declares:

Those years were a singular phenomenon in the life of our nation. Spain beat like an enormous heart, within an immense, nearly impermeable shell, almost outside the life of the rest of humanity. But within that isolation and a tone of modest provincialism that infiltrated into the whole nation, one can be certain that there have been few times when the soul of a people achieved such plenitude, so profound a realization of what it ought to be.[10]

The difficulty lies in drawing a dividing line between the parts of this appreciation that are merely nostalgic and those that are real. There is no doubt that in this case nostalgia – always insidious and distorting – has influenced Marañón's judgment. The calamitous period of 1936–1939 could only serve to make the relative calm of the preceding decades look greater than it was, by simple contrast. No more than relative, be it understood, because the sixty years between the Restoration and the Civil War are not lacking in unfortunate incidents: the loss of the colonies, the 'Tragic Week' in Barcelona, revolutionary strikes, anarchist attacks, the ill-fated campaign in Morocco, etc. Even in Azorín, who made so many sharp comments about the Restoration, we can see a desire to rectify his previous criticisms after the Spanish Civil War. In 1939 he wrote, in Paris, an evocation of the Madrid of half a century before, laden with the same 'inexpressible melancholy' felt by Marañón, the melancholy that comes when a past is definitively lost, a past one tries to recapture through the corridors of memory or the magic of the daydream: the Madrid of Lagartijo, of Vico, of Campoamor and Núñez de Arce, of Galdós and Menéndez Pelayo. Using his character Damián Olivares as his mouthpiece, Azorín says:

The present is this present and no other. The present is the time of fifty years ago and not today's time. . . It is not true that any past time was better. There is only one time. And the past is the only one. And it is the only one because our personality is rooted in it. But in addition, in this case of mine, that period in the history of Spain in which I, Damián Olivares, have developed, is marvelous.[11]

And lastly, in 1941, Azorín speaks openly of 'the splendid sixty years of the Alfonsine Restoration'.[12] In a quarter of a century he went from critical denial to sentimental affirmation of that period so often disputed by all sides.

2. Confessions of a child of the times

During the summer of 1876 a little volume entitled *Minuta de un testamento* made its appearance in Madrid bookstores.[13] The title was certainly not one of those that irresistibly capture the ordinary reader's attention; and, in fact, the book would certainly have gone unnoticed had it not been for the extraordinary circumstance that, in the place where the author's name ought to be, the eye was caught by an exotic letter W followed by several dots. And another circumstance that aroused curiosity was the fact that the *Revista Europea*, usually not much interested in criticism of books, published a review of the *Minuta* in October of that year which, owing to its length, had to be printed in two successive numbers of the weekly magazine.[14] To the anonymous status of the *Minuta*'s author was added the semi-anonymity represented by the initials J. C. with which the unusual review was signed. There is no doubt that the reviewer knew the identity of W..., despite the fact that he remarked jocosely, 'We do not care to discover the author's name that is hidden under the letter W..., indecipherable for us, for *Wenceslao* Ayguals de Izco is dead, we were unaware that General *Weyler* is dedicated to this kind of study, and of the Baroness *Wilson* we know that she does not profess the high-minded doctrines found in this remarkable document.'[15] Nor is there any doubt that many persons shared the secret. A manuscript version of the *Minuta* had been circulating in Madrid for several months.[16] Though it did not exactly contain subversive doctrines, the book suggested viewpoints not likely to be favorably received in official circles during the early months of the Restoration. The manuscript had passed from hand to hand, therefore, among people who sympathized with the author's opinions and to whom he was certainly no stranger. Once the printed version was published, no one tried very hard to keep a secret that had never been more than a convention. Behind the W...hid, or pretended to hide, Gumersindo de Azcárate, who had recently returned to Madrid from a year of exile in Cáceres. As for the review published in the *Revista Europea*, it was soon learned that it came from the pen of a young lawyer named Joaquín Costa, a former pupil of Azcárate's at the University of Madrid. And it was precisely in that year, 1876, that the reviewer had published the initial work in a long series of juridical, historical, and social studies. That work was entitled *La vida del derecho.*

At the risk of adding one more to the list of contradictory comments

on the Restoration, we must summarize the amalgam of novel, auto-
biography, and catechism which, at first sight, the *Minuta de un
testamento* appears to be. First of all, the book possesses the interest of
having been written after the return of the Bourbons, when the hopes
that had been centered on the young Alfonso XII had prevailed against
the suspicions of the anti-dynastic faction. But here a warning must be
issued. The author of the *Minuta* could hardly be expected to have an
impartial opinion about the Spain of Alfonso XII, and much less about
Cánovas's first government. In the first place Azcárate was a republican.
In the second, it must not be forgotten that he was one of the professors
who had been removed from their chairs because they had refused to
comply with the measures contained in the Royal Decree of 26
February 1875. We can surmise that, in the first place, the Restoration
had a literal meaning for Azcárate: it was the re-establishment, not only
of a discredited dynasty, but also a restoration of the corrupt politics
and arbitrary actions of Isabella II's Spain. Certainly it had been an
arbitrary act to confine Francisco Giner in the castle of Santa Catalina
in Cádiz, and Laureano Calderón and Augusto González de Linares in
the castle of San Antón in La Coruña, and to deport Nicolás Salmerón
to Lugo and Azcárate himself to Cáceres. Part of the *Minuta* had been
written in the Extremaduran capital. And yet it is astonishing that a
work conceived under such conditions should be totally free of resentment and invective. Discretion of style and moderation of ideas are its
most characteristic traits. Menéndez Pelayo, disconcerted precisely
because of its absence of polemics, called it 'a work of insidious gentle-
ness'.[17]

When we turn the pages of this curious little book a number of
questions come to mind. The first has to do with the title. What led
Azcárate to clothe his thoughts in the guise of a fictitious will? But if we
reflect for a moment we will see that, in fact, what we have before us is
the retrospective view of a whole epoch, an epoch characterized by a
peculiar way of thinking about and sensing human reality and, more
narrowly, Spanish reality; an epoch, moreover, which the fictional
testator thinks has come to its end. That epoch can be described as
liberal, reformist, and freethinking. It is not difficult to set the chronological events that begin and end it. Its beginning is to be found in the
Revolution of 1854, a late Spanish temblor of the European revolutionary earthquake of 1848. It is true that this revolution had features
of a barracks uprising and a small-scale mutiny, but it also possessed an
undeniable ideological side, lent to it by the participation of the bud-

ding intellectual class. 'During that two-year period,' wrote Menéndez Pelayo, 'began to flower the hopes of a more radical faction which recruited its members among the youth who had recently emerged from the teachings of the university's ideologues and economists'.[18] It must be remembered, as a not unimportant detail, that in that same year of 1854 Sanz del Río put an end to his years of study in retirement at Illescas and rejoined the University of Madrid as professor of History of Philosophy. The end of the epoch is clear: it is marked by the Restoration.

Azcárate's intention is to give an account of those twenty years, 1854–1874; it was a period he had viewed from the watchtower of adversity, and full of the desires, hopes, and disenchantments of a true 'child of the times'. For in Azcárate the characteristic traits of his time find full expression. That is why the *Minuta* is such a valuable source for understanding the psychology of those twenty years. It is a *testimony* as well as a *testament*, a faithful description of the past with an eye to its vindication in the future; for the recommendations and warnings offered by the fictional testator to those who will receive his inheritance – that is, to all Spaniards – have no other purpose but this. 'That general examination of conscience', writes the author in the preface, 'is a tribute paid to sincerity, which does not allow man to go down to posterity honored more than he deserves or vilified more than he ought to be, and moreover as an example which should be instructive for everyone; and so the life of one man contributes to the perfecting of all men's lives.'[19] The *Minuta* arises from the critical introversion that accompanies a grave personal crisis. In a most unhappy phase of his life, Azcárate feels an irresistible desire to string his memories together, to link them in such a way that the resulting chain will give them a very important meaning. And nothing could be more natural. When the life around us seems presided over by unreason and contingency, when an uncrossable chasm is opened between what the world *is* and what we expect it to be, reaction is not long in coming. External confusion is the spur that impels us toward greater internal cohesion. And so we try to make the elements of our inner life arrange themselves in disciplined rows that allow us to see at a glance the assets on which we can count to alleviate our feeling of helplessness.

In the *Minuta*, therefore, Azcárate collects and arranges all his thoughts on matters of importance: religion, law, politics, pedagogy, sociology, ethics, etc. If we take the author's ideological position into account we will see how useful the book is in understanding the

Krausist way of looking at certain questions, especially some which, though always open to controversy, are all the more so during times when there is a desire to revise traditional values. But the *Minuta* is something more than a recapitulation of thoughts and personal memories. Every Krausist is, almost by definition, a missionary *in partibus infidelium*, and in Azcárate the desire for persuasion is almost as lively as in Sanz del Río, his teacher, though somewhat less obvious. The little volume fulfills two functions, (a) that of clearing the author and his fellow Krausists of the accusations that had been made against them for years and renewed under the Restoration; and (b) that of placing in the common reader's hands a short and simple description not of Krausism's doctrinal substance but the life of a Krausist. And it was presented in the form of an inner dialogue, skillfully avoiding polemics, as if the author, bent on nothing more than pondering his thoughts one by one, wanted to show that it was not eccentricity, passion, or mere chance, but reflection and love for truth that had led him to adopt or reject this or that ideological position.

The autobiographical nature of a large part of the *Minuta* is beyond question, though in some passages the author tries, for concealment's sake, to throw the reader off the track by introducing some fictitious detail. This happens, for example, with the portrait he offers of his father. Apart from the fact that this worthy man named Patricio de Azcárate was not a physician, as the *Minuta* states, but a lawyer, the rest of the picture faithfully reflects certain unmistakable traits of Azcárate's father:

My father, born into the middle class, was a physician by profession, and perhaps for this reason a supporter of the scientific and religious movement with which the present century began in our country. Under the inspiration of French philosophy and the Revolution of 1789, he had abandoned in his heart of hearts the religious beliefs of his forebears and had embraced enthusiastically and wholeheartedly the new political ideas, serving them unselfishly and patriotically and submitting, with regard to them, to the almost necessary hypocrisy which the times in a sense forced upon him.[20]

But, as is well known, Patricio de Azcárate was more than a mere amateur of the French encyclopaedists. He wrote very respectable critical works on history and philosophy, especially his *Exposición histórico-crítica de los sistemas filosóficos modernos* (1861), apparently composed to serve as a guide for his son, who at the time was finishing his studies at the University of Madrid. And not content with this, he was the founder and editor of the *Biblioteca filosófica* where, beginning in 1866, twenty-six volumes of classic works of philosophy were published. The writings of Plato, Aristotle, and Leibniz in that collection were translated and had introductions and notes by Don Patricio himself. This may be the explanation for his son's early preference for speculative studies, as well as the slant taken by his political and religious ideas. But the most valuable legacy that Gumersindo received from his father was psychological rather than ideological: a calm and untroubled attitude toward life, an attitude that showed itself in an indestructible equanimity and a scrupulous respect for any sincerely professed idea or belief. It is surprising today to observe the genuine deference with which his adversaries, even the bitterest of them, treated him. Over and above any disagreement they admired the honorable, noble, and simple man who, as Ortega says, left all around him 'a vast murmur of ideal enthusiasms, a warm gust of esential patriotism, and surpassing humanity'.[21]

3. Nineteenth-century Spanish liberalism

The portion of the *Minuta* devoted to politics is a sort of compendium of the development and conduct of a nineteenth-century Spanish liberal. Spanish liberalism before the September Revolution was bifaceted: it had one doctrinaire and utopian aspect, and another that was turbulent and emotional. And there is nothing strange about this, for it was the stepchild both of eighteenth-century rationalism and the convulsions of the great romantic upheaval. 'Several causes contributed', writes Azcárate, 'to my professing liberal ideas. In the first place they were those of my father, who had suffered difficulties and persecutions because of them; and then, both by instinct and temperament, absolutism repelled me.'[22] He received the theoretical basis from his father, an avid reader and collector of books of French philosophy; but his enthusiasms are those of a man who, unmistakably inclined toward romanticism, seeks examples in history of the struggle between freedom and despotism. When he was still a youngster Gumersindo had enjoyed reading about those episodes in the history of Spain which dramatized that struggle: the Councils of Toledo, the oath sworn by the kings of Aragon to preserve existing rights and privileges, the war of the *comuneros* (1520–1521). However, the subject that most engaged his emotions was the fight against Bourbon absolutism: 'all the uprisings

that took place in the first third of this century to establish a constitutional regime appealed to my sympathies, and the names of the men
who took part in them were, for me, the names of heroes and martyrs'.[23]
During his youthful years, it was at the university that his predilection
for political liberalism was confirmed. Fiction comes into his story only
in one detail: the testator says that he has studied medicine. In fact, it
was law. During the years between the Revolution of 1854 and that of
1868, the Faculty of Medicine was the focus from which spread ideas
hostile to any type of absolutism. Azcárate states:

> It is a fact that both then and later almost all physicians were liberals.
> Censorship, which impeded circulation of any book that might oppose the
> religious and political principles of the old regime, did not stop to think
> that the books of medicine that were sent us from beyond the Pyrenees
> contained rather more than what was necessary to make experts in the art
> of healing. Hence for many years, and even today, Spanish physicians have
> been materialists and liberals...

Less fortunate were the lawyers who, unable to use a similar subterfuge,
'steeped themselves in the doctrines that they learned secretly and with
great caution in the books which, despite all the government's pre-
cautions, came into their hands'.[24]

Azcárate's political trajectory can be inferred from the statements he
attributes to his testator. An ardent constitutionalist, he embraced the
cause of Isabella II. His aversion to absolutism led him to be active in
the ranks of the most radical liberal party, the progressivists, for 'with
affirmation of the people's sovereignty, with disentailment and expro-
priation of Church property, even when they [the progressivists] were
not always successful in conceiving and carrying out these principles
and reforms, they destroyed the old regime's political and social organization'.[25] He always refused to be a deputy to the Cortes, even when
very favorable conditions were offered him, but he did accept the offices
of alderman and provincial deputy. He often engaged in conspiracies,
like almost every nineteenth-century Spanish liberal. He participated in
the Revolution of 1868 and claimed to be proud of having done so,
despite the fact that in the course of time he had gradually lost faith in
the effectiveness of movements involving force; but he insists that
'insurrection is a right when the people have recourse to this means
after all hope of using peaceful means has been lost, in order to recover
their sovereignty and be masters of their fate, wresting power from the
hands of an institution or minority which has exercised it abusively and
tyrannically'.[26] As for his political activity during the years immediately

following the Revolution, the account he gives of it is sufficiently condensed to enable me to quote it in its entirety:

During the years from 1868 to 1875 I was affiliated with the most liberal
party within the Monarchy; I accepted Prince Amadeo of Savoy; I
deplored the way in which both conservatives and members of my own
party behaved toward him; when he abdicated, I did not approve of the
way the Republic was proclaimed, although, realizing that there had to be
a choice between this solution and Restoration [of the monarchy], I was
one of those who accepted the former solution in good faith; I viewed with
sorrow the criminal cantonal movement, with repugnance the show of
force on 2 January 1874, and without surprise that of 31 December of the
same year.[27]

But if the Restoration did not catch him by surprise, he harbored no
illusions about it either. He admitted unconditionally that in Spain the
only conceivable dynasty was that of the Bourbons, but foresaw unhappy consequences for the country in this very exclusivity. He found
extremely unconvincing the promises of tolerance and concord trum-
peted by the politicians. Had he not been ejected from his university
chair and exiled from his home by those who spoke of conciliation?
The government of the restored monarchy continued to exercise semi-
dictatorial powers, under which it wove the web of deceit known as the
Constitution of 1876. But the fictitious constitutionalism sponsored by
Cánovas was inevitable. The Restoration had to give full satisfaction to
those who had made it possible, and naturally they tried to make it into
an instrument of spurious interests. 'For fear of losing a power that is
slipping out of their hands', writes Azcárate, 'the men in charge of the
situation use and wield the means that chance has placed in their hands,
in works that serve not to procure the country's good but to satisfy the
demands of this or that individual.'[28] If proclamation of the first Republic had been an act of political insanity, the Restoration had been something still worse, an act of force which, in the vain desire to purge itself
of its congenital illegality, created an *ad hoc* legality which was not even
respected, but floated in the void, weightless and spectral, like the
emanation from a putrefying corpse. Azcárate says that he feels no
antipathy toward Alfonso XII, and that perhaps the king intends to
rule constitutionally. But in the long run it will not be the young king
who decides the direction Spanish politics is going to take, but 'politicians who are self-seeking and short-sighted, if not egotistical and ill-
intentioned', from whose influence he will try in vain to extricate
himself. And even recognizing that nothing prevented the monarchy

from being 'expansive, tolerant, respectful of the law', nothing indicated, early in 1876, that it intended to be so.[29]

Because of all this the testator declares himself to be a supporter of the
Republic:

> but not of the individualistic, narrow, and senseless Republic of those who,
> paying pagan worship to mere form, imagine that they have everything
> when they have that kind of Republic; nor the revolutionary and dis-
> organizing Republic of those who are trying to revive the class struggle
> and solve in one day delicate questions which demand deliberation and
> maturity of judgment; but the Republic that is at once reformist and
> conservative.[30]

4. Stability and flexibility

This is, in substance, the *Minuta*'s political content. There is really
nothing very remarkable about it. Azcárate's political ideas coincide
with those of intellectual and moderate nineteenth-century liberalism.
But we need not stress overmuch something which is, in fact, only an
apparent coincidence. Indeed, the political orientation of the *Minuta*'s
author must not be considered in isolation but in close relationship with
an overall ideology. Stated in different terms, Azcárate is a liberal
because political liberalism is a necessary postulate of Krause's doctrine;
for by insisting that there is no other authority than that of reason
Krause stresses the fact that the free exercise of reason is impossible
under a political regime founded on Caesarism or arbitrariness. And so,
for Azcárate and his fellow Krausists, to say 'liberalism' is the same as
saying 'political projection of harmonic rationalism', and to fight for
the first of these is to help to implant the second. After all, had not
Krause himself given proof of it when he came out in defense of liberalism during his years of teaching in Göttingen? The Krausist did not
embrace liberalism out of simple preference or whim, but because he
had necessarily to be a liberal if he wished to remain faithful to the
spirit of the doctrine he professed.[31]

Of course the Spanish Krausists' political activities had to be adjusted, as is evident from the *Minuta*, to the conditions imposed by
historical circumstance. The practical nature of the doctrine suggested
the desirability of making use, in politics as in every other sphere, of
existing institutions, using and modifying them to the advantage of the
new ideal's future triumph. Like the testator, the Krausist thought he
ought to support Isabella II because, in spite of a multitude of reprehensible actions, he saw better hopes for the liberal cause in those of her

political persuasion than in the absolutism of the pretender, Don Carlos. He accepted Amadeo of Savoy because there was an implicit promise of constitutionalism in the new dynasty. After Amadeo's abdication he preferred the republic to the monarchy because the latter, in Spain, embodied a tradition of irresponsible personal power from which any future occupant of the throne would find it very hard to dissociate himself. But basically, Krausist moderation continued to work toward a political system that would combine maximum stability with maximum flexibility. In a regime of this kind every change would take the form of a slow and peaceful evolution, the necessary outcome of a combination of organic possibilities, rather than the alteration resulting from obstacles or shocks originating outside the regime. In a system based on moderation, compromise, and mutual respect, the distinction between monarchy and republic would cease to have the exaggerated importance it was given in Spain, for reasons as clear as they were lamentable. Azcárate always showed a special predilection for the British monarchy where, as an expert in political science, he could study the change in institutions of a people who were as anxious to preserve individual freedom as to assure social equilibrium. In a country like England revolution is inconceivable; still more, it would be a crime, and the revolutionary would deserve to be treated like a common criminal who would commit a crime against his fellow citizens, the only repositories of effective sovereignty.[32] But Spain is not England, and it is to Spaniards that the following observation is addressed:

If...the monarch...cherishes the idea of exercising permanently the supreme and almost unlimited power he has, and, for the same reason, opposes everything that tends toward sharing that power with the people and preparing them to exercise it; if he considers the nation, in the manner of absolute kings, as something that is placed at the service of his personal interest or that of his family...if he does not use the existence of political parties for any other purpose than to give a constitutional and parliamentary varnish to the Government, which is at bottom and in fact purely personal...then revolution will come as a just punishment, and as an effective and sole possible remedy for such a state of affairs.[33]

The intent of these words, written during the early months of the Restoration, is unmistakable.

Spirit of controversy

1. Hostility to Krausism

After 1854, the year when Sanz del Río returned to teaching, the Krausist doctrine was forced to live in an atmosphere of constant controversy. The weapons of ridicule, invective, and intransigence were wielded against Krausism, and when these were not enough the intervention of governmental authority was relied upon to limit the spread of a way of thinking whose rapid growth seemed to threaten serious dangers to religion, the State, and society. The most stubborn opposition came from the so-called neo-Catholic group, which assumed the defense of Catholicism against the secularizing tendencies – when it did not think of them as openly anti-ecclesiastical or anticlerical – of liberal democracy.[1] Zealously opposed to everything that might mean an abridgement of the Church's traditional rights, neo-Catholicism looked with favor on the theories of de Maistre and Bonald, associated itself with the cause of the pretender Don Carlos, and believed that it had found moral support in Pope Pius IX's antiliberal and antiprogressivist campaign. The combativeness of this movement, spearheaded by laymen, found effective expression in the periodical press, in a kind of inflammatory journalism which did not hesitate to descend to the level of 'politics of the barricades', a journalism that was, in fact, very typical of the nineteenth century.[2] The model for this class of publications was the Paris daily newspaper *L'Univers*, whose editor, Louis Veuillot, was in his turn the prototype of the neo-Catholic journalist. A task similar to that carried out in France by Veuillot was aspired to, in Spain, by Francisco Navarro Villoslada with the evening newspaper *El Pensamiento Español*, founded in Madrid by Gabino Tejado in 1860.[3]

Hostility toward Krausism, which had been unfocused during the decade that followed Sanz del Río's return to university teaching, reached a peak during the three-year span 1865–1867. Navarro Villoslada opened this period of maximum abuse in March, 1865, demanding that the government expel those holders of university chairs who, in their written or oral teaching, insulted religion and the monarchy. One after another the heterodox and subversive professors were paraded through the columns of *El Pensamiento Español*: Sanz del Río and Fernando de Castro, Castelar and Canalejas, Giner and Figuerola, and a number of others, were denounced as *living texts*: that is, as incarnations of disruptive doctrines. The anti-Krausist campaign eventually overflowed the boundaries of the periodical press, invaded the Cortes, rose to government level, and inspired the decree of 22 January 1867, which obliged professors to swear an oath of allegiance to Church and Throne. The Royal Order of 30 May of the same year expelled from their chairs all those who, in defense of academic freedom, refused to comply with this repressive requirement. It might be said that the secular arm finished, in its own fashion, what the ecclesiastical authority had begun in its fashion in September, 1865, when it placed Sanz del Río's *Ideal de la Humanidad* on the Roman Index.

But in fact neither Navarro Villoslada's stentorian campaign nor the denunciatory writings of Orti y Lara, Moreno Nieto, Caminero, Torres Vélez, and others, nor the persecution of the professors who followed Krause's doctrines, had more than a secondary interest. For those who attacked Krausism on the eve of the Revolution of 1868 did so not for intellectual reasons but for political and religious ones, in the measure in which religion can be the instrument of politics or politics of religion. It is undeniable that Krausism's enemies triumphed in the end, but we would do well to emphasize the fact that their victory was owed not to superior intelligence or subtlety, or even the merits of the cause for which they fought. They owed it simply to the support of governmental authority, that irresistible fulminator of arbitrary dismissals and suspensions. In 1867 Narváez personified the panic of a policy that was at its last gasp, and hence given to stupid and absurd repressions. With such a policy, indeed, absolutely nothing could be solved. Still, it had a certain exemplary value. Another conservative politician, Cánovas, would learn from it what not to do. And it is not strange that, having seen the disastrous results of such a policy on another person, the architect of the Restoration should have craftily and gradually withdrawn – after a prelude of apparent compromise – from the extreme kind of traditionalism zealous to stamp out all opposing thought.

But if that hostility of the pre-Revolutionary period lies outside intellectual history, the same cannot be said of the controversies that swirled around Krausism in the early days of the Restoration. These controversies are extraordinarily interesting, and for three chief reasons. The first is that they found expression in periodicals which, aimed at an audience where all ideological shades were represented, maintained a neutral or at least discreet attitude about the subject under discussion. These were the reviews of wide circulation with which we will deal below. In the second place, those who took part in the controversies were important figures in the Spanish intellectual world: Menéndez Pelayo, Campoamor, Laverde, Revilla, Azcárate, Canalejas, Salmerón, Perojo, etc. In the third place, the object of the disputes was something more than deciding whether or not Krausism was a philosophy of immanence and whether it ought to be taught to the university youth of a Catholic country. The controversy often assumed a historical dimension, and at times skirted the area of 'cultural psychology'. In any case, this second wave of controversy centering on Krausism served, in participants as well as spectators, to fix attitudes, prejudices, and aspirations which for a long time to come would feed what has often been called 'the concern for Spain' among her children, mother-lode of all other concerns.

2. Journals of the bourgeoisie

Whoever takes the trouble to leaf through Spanish periodical publications of the period 1865–1880 will be astonished at the breadth of opinion and elevation of tone with which they treat the most diverse questions. Philosophy and religion, physical and natural sciences, sociology and politics, economics and history, literature and art, etc., every sector of human knowledge finds a place in newspaper columns and magazine pages. When domestic production is insufficient to satisfy the reading public's obvious appetite, Spanish publications of the period raid the abundant stocks of European reviews and distribute the booty in the form of versions that are often pedestrian but always well intentioned. A rapid examination of the articles of foreign origin offered to the Spanish reader would reveal that scarcely any French or English journal escaped the systematic pillage. However, something really quite remarkable about the journals of this period is the impartiality with which the most widely contrasting views are presented to the public, on subjects where equanimity is often very hard to achieve. Cardinal Manning shares the reader's attention with Ernest Renan; Monsignor Dupanloup, bishop of Orléans, and Albert Réville, pastor of the Walloon church of Rotterdam, brandish the weapons of persuasion each in his different way; the materialist physicist John Tyndall and the Unitarian theologian James Martineau repeat in the Spanish language a controversy that had caused a great sensation in the English-speaking world. And these were the foreign authors. As for Spanish ones, the neutrality maintained by the periodicals of wide circulation is even more surprising, for controversies within Spain tended to be rather more bitter and personal than those outside the country. Cándido Nocedal, an uncompromising ultramontanist, published in the same journal that printed Gumersindo de Azcárate's latest opinions on ecclesiastical despotism; the traditionalist Manuel Alonso Martínez and the rationalist Francisco de Paula Canalejas shared, at least in principle, the same reading public; and Marcelino Menéndez Pelayo had no objection to publishing his writings in the same place as the Viscount de Torres Solanot, a spiritualist; though elsewhere, and with entire justice, he accused him of plagiarism.

And so it was that periodical publication in Spain – as, of course, in other countries and precisely at the time we are discussing – became the preferred way of placing under public consideration subjects of general interest. But on the other hand, anything can become a subject of general interest simply because the attention of a periodical publication is brought to bear on it. Magazines and newspapers, obviously, have always demonstrated great skill in raising or exacerbating the most varied sorts of problems. They need only to arouse the curiosity of readers and focus it carefully on a particular subject. That such a procedure can lend itself to abuse and deception is something that the art of propaganda has made abundantly clear. However, other means of cultural diffusion employed in modern society run the same risk. The European and American periodicals published after 1850 respond, in the first place, to an elementary quantitative demand – that is, an enormous increase in the number of readers;[4] and in the second place, to a qualitative demand, the avidity for reliable news about the most recent scientific and technical achievements and about the rapid and widespread expansion of the frontiers of knowledge. It is the new middle class, the bourgeoisie – newly liberated and perhaps for that very reason tending toward liberalism – inquisitive and eager for novelty, capricious and iconoclastic, which brought into being those admirable instruments of cultural information that appeared under such names as *Fortnightly Review, Atlantic Monthly, Revue Scientifique, Nuova Antologia, Deutsche Rundschau*, and *Revista de España*.

The *Revista de España*, founded in 1868, forms together with the *Revista Europea*, founded in 1874 and the *Revista Contemporánea* in

1875, the triad of general Spanish reviews which can be compared without apology to the best of their kind in Europe. The date when the first of these saw the light links it to the beginning of the revolutionary interregnum; the second and third mark, respectively, the end of the confusing parenthesis and the beginning of the Restoration. It is to be noted, therefore, that in the short space of seven years three publications of great importance in disseminating modern thought in the Peninsula became established in Spain's cultural life. The fact that all three cluster around the September Revolution is highly significant. All of them proposed to utilize, by guiding it, an intellectual revival of which the revolutionary tumult had been only one phase. The Revolution of 1868 was the rebellion of the Spanish middle class, presided over by the progressive party and indoctrinated by intellectuals brimming with theories and opinions of many kinds. The monarchy dreamed of by Prim and Sagasta when the crown was offered to Amadeo of Savoy was the typical mesocratic and egalitarian monarchy to which nineteenth-century liberalism so ardently – and vainly – aspired. The Republic established in 1873 was inspired by similar desires for liberal moderation, with the difference that, having broken all links with day-to-day reality, it drifted rudderless for a short time and ended by sinking into anarchy. Both the monarchy of Savoy and the first republic owed their failure, among other causes, to the weakness and political confusion of the middle class that had brought them into being. The September Revolution, with its train of theorizers, philanthropists, and dreamers, tried to take advantage of the European bourgeoisie's conquests, ratified by the social and political structure that had emerged from the uprisings of 1848. But it was a useless endeavour. The class that gave the Revolution its most prominent figures was a still rudimentary social stratum in Spain, unable owing to its small numbers to impose its standards on the rest of the country. The ease with which they had overthrown Isabella II's monarchy had given the middle-class politicians of 1868 an exaggerated notion of their own strength. They did not stop to think that the monarchy, which had been steadily undermined over a long period, had collapsed almost without the need of a push from without. It was not the strength of the middle class, but the common people's disaffection and the aristocracy's ineptness that had really caused the downfall of the monarchical institution. For the middle class did not become a social force in Spain until well after establishment of the Restoration. And even so its scope, influence, and power have always been much less than those of the bourgeoisie in the rest of Europe.

But the Spanish bourgeoisie, as a cultural body if not as a class, began to disseminate its ideals long before it was able to intervene successfully in national life. The three periodicals we have mentioned, all of them bourgeois creations, stressed beliefs and ideas dear to the middle class. All three were liberal, humanitarian, freethinking, and internationalist – which did not prevent each one, however, from having a particular ideological cast. The *Revista de España* embodied the attitudes of the Spanish liberal group of 1812, and was perhaps the one with the broadest and most balanced viewpoint. The *Revista Europea*, though it was not exactly a Krausist organ, did show a certain preference for harmonic rationalism and included some prominent disciples of Sanz del Río among its contributors. The *Revista Contemporánea*, during the years when it was edited by José del Perojo, inclined toward neo-Kantianism with some touches of positivism, whose teachings it spread with considerable vigor.[5] In short, all three were hostile to traditionalism, to narrow and intransigent cultural nationalism, and to ultramontanism. And no study of nineteenth-century intellectual Spain is possible without a careful examination of these publications and a judgment about the influence they exercised.

3. History as an offensive weapon

The journal, less ephemeral than the daily newspaper and more ubiquitous and accessible than the book, serves as an excellent vehicle for intellectual controversy. And if it is observed, in addition, that the Spanish journals to which we have referred sprang from the upheavals of a revolutionary – and hence revisionary – period, it is not strange that they displayed the tensions characteristic of minds rendered hypersensitive by discord. The subject of discussion during the years of the September Revolution and the early Restoration was not only Spain's present and future but also what interpretation to give to the historical trajectory described by the country. There is nothing coincidental about the fact that the angriest controversies arising during that period rested on a historical base. By this we do not mean that the role played by ideas should be disdained, but rather that any idea – or belief, or judgment – is linked from the outset to a particular historical moment. The men of 1868 were ardent historicists. The historical element filtered into everything: into the novel with Galdós, into poetry with Núñez de Arce, into painting with Pradilla, into literary and aesthetic studies with Menéndez Pelayo, into law with Costa, into religion with Canalejas, etc.

The most prominent political figures – Castelar, Cánovas, Pi y Margall – assiduously cultivated history. Not even the *coup d'état* of Sagunto on 29 December 1874 escaped the contemporary enthusiasm for history. The Restoration's chief task, we might say, was to tie up the loose ends of time, for that seems to be the meaning of 're-establishing Spain's historical continuity'. And even among the anonymous mass, terms like 'tradition' and 'progress', which the contending factions aimed at each other like projectiles, were loaded with temporal – that is, historical – significance.

One characteristic of controversies is that they shed light on the participants and darkness on the subject under debate. Today, as we carefully re-read the intellectual diatribes of the Restoration's early years, we observe two things. The first is that, as far as proof or rejection of the theses under discussion is concerned, the result is totally sterile. No one convinces anyone, perhaps because the polemicist seeks to persuade his adversary rather less strenuously than to persuade himself. The writer who wields his pen like a spur or whip – Unamuno or Larra, for example, among many others – is often a victim of his own insecurity, an unsatisfied and yearning soul who transmutes his inner disturbances into aggression. In the second place, we see that rarely have such peculiar interpretations been offered of Spain's past – her political, religious, social, and intellectual past – as during that period. The 'philosophy of history' – that art of prophesying about the past, as Juan Valera said – was the order of the day. Some on a larger scale, some on a smaller, every person with pretensions to culture thought he could see clearly into the dark meaning of past events and, armed with the guarantee offered by that pretended knowledge, judged the present and the future with breathtaking impertinence.

But there is a further factor, and it is that in most cases this polemical use of history disguised a militant dislike for contemporary life. In reality it is an attitude similar to that which makes man court utopia, which means that it too is a way of escaping from the unpleasantness of the present. However, it does not really resemble a utopia. What is utopian is the quintessentially rational and generic. The paradises it builds are geometrical structures peopled by pure concepts. What is historical, however, embodies the irrational and specific. The use of history as an instrument of controversy, characteristic of the early days of the Restoration, demonstrates the rebellion, among the educated class, of past and future against the present, of traditionalism and progressivism against the Spain of the day. What was in fact scorned was the Spain of the day, sometimes in the name of past greatness and sometimes in that of an imagined future glory. The most notable polemicists were either champions of tradition like Menéndez Pelayo and Laverde or proponents of progress like Perojo and Revilla.

Nor is it superfluous to note another aspect that was a little less superficial than the historicism which concealed the rebellion of 'yesterday' and 'tomorrow' against 'today', namely, the man of passion's hatred for the man of ideas, the *esprit de finesse* against the *esprit de géométrie*, or, in simpler terms, the man who has 'reasons' against the man who possesses 'reason'. A considerable part of Spanish intellectual life in the revolutionary period was dominated by the ideologues of Krausism. All of them were untiring planners, and in proof of this there still exist the innumerable plans, blueprints, and models with which they intended to rebuild Spain in the image and likeness of harmonic rationalism. As devotees of reason they had a distorted notion of what was historical. History for them was not the temporal projection of human life but the realization of an idea in time. Considered in itself, this idea has no other value than that of illustrating the relationship which man maintains, at a given instant, with God and with humanity; or, in other words, the value of measuring the distance which at that instant separates life as reality from life as ideal, of separating what *is* from what *ought to be*. But this, after all, implies the distortion of history. History feeds only on what *is* at a given moment, and the historian's job consists in asking how and why what *is* has *come to be*. Everything else simply means subjecting history to utopia, life to reason. Reason does in fact build an image of full, perfect man. Life reveals to us imperfect man, though in principle he is capable of correcting his deficiencies. For the Krausist, history is the chronicle of that gradual and actual correction. The harmonic rationalist reviews history to see at what distance from the target of perfection the human archer plants his arrow at any given moment.

All this simply means that the Krausists, like the ideocrats of every period, are unskilled historians. Nor can it be said of them that they interpret history after their own fashion, that is, filling it with their personal prejudices, passions, and designs. That would be natural and tolerable. But the fact is that they do not interpret it according to anyone's fashion. That harmonic reason on which they call as a court of last appeal is, of course, abstract and has no owner, the sort of reason which, because it is everyone's, belongs to no one; and that man, a perfect being because a reasonable being, is a theoretical man, geo-metrically constructed; in short, an unborn man, a non-man.

The historian's rebellion against the ideologue is a sign that, once the theorizing and utopian spirit is discredited by revolution, concrete man at last takes his revenge. Reason is again torn apart by unreason, by life, exactly as the Mayan temple is destroyed by the jungle exuber-ance around it. And the polemical debates which accompany this phenomenon bring to the surface the disillusionment, on the one hand, and the irritations, on the other, left behind by every revolutionary period.

4. Significance of the 'reaction' under Cánovas

In December, 1875, scarcely a year after the uprising in Sagunto, Manuel de la Revilla wrote:

> Here...there is hardly any sign of intellectual activity...In Madrid there is intellectual life only in the Athenaeum, in the Academy of Jurispru-dence, and in the Spanish Society of Natural History...Years ago a famous man...brought to Spain the spirit of German philosophy and gave new life to our thought...Foci of this movement [Krausism] were the University and the Madrid Athenaeum; the former is no longer such a focus, for reasons that need not be gone into here, but in the latter the philosophical tradition of the last few years is still maintained...Political life in Spain and the life of the Athenaeum are in inverse ratio to each other.[6]

This diagnosis, though undoubtedly biased, is however substantially correct. It is true that the early months of the Restoration were characterized by repression of the intellectuals considered hostile to the new state of affairs. Manuel de Orovio was back in the Ministry of Public Works, and the University of Madrid, from which he expelled the most recalcitrant professors, had subsided into the routine teaching of superficial knowledge. Even Manuel de la Revilla himself, among whose virtues circumspection was certainly not included, skillfully evaded the subject of persecution in the universities. Was this a theatrical gesture? Was it a studied tactic from a man who was soon to aspire to the Chair of General and Spanish Literature at the University of Madrid? We do not know for sure. Six months previously, when he came out in defense of the persecuted Krausists against Campoamor's absurd attacks, the young critic had alluded to 'certain measures by the ministry of Cánovas which I cannot discuss here, for probably I would not have the same freedom for defense which you [Campoamor] have so much of for attack'.[7] Those measures were, of course, the ones taken by Orovio against the professors who had refused to comply with the Royal Decree of 26 February 1875. It is obvious that Revilla was trying to give the impression that the air of Madrid was unhealthy for those who did not approve the government's actions with regard to the Krausist professors. Their departure meant that the University of Madrid was bled white. The Athenaeum, on the other hand, continued to enjoy its customary privilege of free examination and free discussion. Everything in the 'learned House' demonstrated an activity even greater than was normal. The intellectual tendencies that had been suppressed in official teaching centers took refuge and entrenched themselves there. As usual, the corridors and meeting rooms were the scene of heated verbal jousting on all questions, divine and human. Indeed, it was during the winter of 1875–1876 that an impassioned debate was held in the section of moral and political sciences: 'Whether the present-day movement of the natural and philosophical sciences in a positivist direction constitutes a grave danger for the great moral, social, and religious principles on which civilization rests.' Revilla himself often took part in the numerous and prolonged discussions about this subject; José Moreno Nieto opposed him; and on this occasion we hear for the first time about an impetuous group of young men, among them positivists like Simarro, Cortezo, Ustáriz, and Morales Díaz, and naturalists like Vicuña, Magaz, and Vicent. Krausism's first rank was, of course, in exile.

But if the 'worthy corporation' served as sanctuary for doctrines that were reputed subversive, and hence exercised a special function, the kind of 'repression' resorted to by Cánovas's ministry must also appear somewhat special. Those punitive measures were not applied to a cultural society which had given the September Revolution its most conspicuous figures, and among whose individual members the restored monarchy surely had more adversaries than sympathizers. For the members of the Athenaeum did not leave their political preferences at the door. Politics both high and low had always been practiced in the Athenaeum, and the 'House' had been notable ever since its foundation for its liberal inclinations, which, more or less accentuated according to the times, had usually pushed it toward the left of whatever official policy was in force. But, despite provocations and resentments, Cánovas left intact the special 'extraterritoriality' of the famous institution and confined his reprisals to those university professors – almost all of them Athenaeum members – who had refused to comply with the terms of the Royal Decree of 25 February 1875. It is superfluous to observe that, by requiring professors to submit their plans of study and textbooks to governmental inspection, the Decree violated the principle of academic freedom of which the professors of Krausist persuasion were particularly zealous defenders. It was a deplorable measure, no matter how justified it may have seemed at the time. And yet, considered from the viewpoint of our own day, when merciless repressions are the rule, Cánovas's reaction seems extremely moderate and even indulgent, in the political as well as the intellectual sphere.

Moreover, it was short-lived. The spring of 1876 brought a moderation of the official attitude with regard to the politicians and intellectuals who had been implicated in the events of 1868–1874 or simply hostile to the Restoration. The professors who had been exiled from Madrid left their places of confinement on the periphery of the country and returned, if not to their chairs – that would not happen until 1881 – at least to their homes in the capital. Giner de los Ríos and his friends were planning to establish the *Institución Libre de Enseñanza* (Free Institution of Education). The liberal spirit, in large part purged of fanaticism but with the memory of its recent failure still fresh, arose again after the discouragement and dejection it had displayed during the first few months of the new situation. The Constitution of 1876 incorporated some of the fundamental aspirations of liberalism, though with many limitations. The change in atmosphere can be observed by comparing Alarcón's novel *El escándalo*, published in 1875, with Galdós's *Doña Perfecta*, which appeared in 1876. People had been separated for a long time by the chasm of the civil wars and political dissension, but they gradually became accustomed to the relative harmony presided over by the restored monarchy. Dialogue was reestablished among the factions, punctuated from time to time by sarcastic comments or vituperation but on the whole tending to mend the tragic rents in the body politic. For be it noted that controversy, no matter how harsh, is after all a form of dialogue.

5. Campoamor, or reprisals

Nowhere is the atmosphere of the Restoration better reflected than in a famous debate provoked by Ramón de Campoamor on 2 May 1875. To see the Asturian versifier striking a blow in favor of an antiliberal cause was not surprising. As early as the winter of 1856–1857 he had made spirited attacks on democracy which had earned him – apart from the antidemocratic faction's immediate applause – the affection of conservatives in general, an affection that remained unsullied by his later fickleness. But to see him breaching a friend's trust in order to satisfy private vengeance in public was something new; as new as seeing him whip up popular wrath against men who had serenely faced misfortune in order to preserve their convictions intact. The soul of Ramón de Campoamor – a very shallow soul – requires something more than summary attention. Observation of it allows us to plumb the moral depths of one intemperate faction of nineteenth-century Spanish conservatism.

Exactly a month after Francisco Giner de los Ríos was exiled to Cádiz, Campoamor sent to the *Revista Europea* a preface he had written for *Dudas y tristezas*, a book of poems by Manuel de la Revilla.[8] This preface was of a very unusual kind, as is proved by the fact that the journal, to dissociate itself from all responsibility, felt obliged to state in a note that 'there is a point [in it] which we might call a current one, and about which we suppose that a tempest of discussion will arise, and it is [the writer's] manner of judging Krausism... and we hope that the defenders of this system will hasten to participate in a discussion for which the *Revista Europea* opens its columns from now on'. The journal's editors were not wrong in their supposition. Campoamor's preface is, as a presentation of Revilla, impertinent; as a literary study it is vulgar; and as an evaluation of Krausism it is malevolent, with a malevolence further heightened by the music-hall humor with which he tries to disguise it. But there is more, and it is that Campoamor caused his preface to be printed in a well-known journal before publication of Revilla's book and without notifying the author in advance. It almost seemed as if the preface's author was afraid that future sales of *Dudas y tristezas* would not suffice to give it the desired publicity. If this was his motive, he was right. Revilla's poetic gifts were extremely slight. The public was hardly going to rush to tear from bookshop shelves the five hundred copies of Revilla's book that were eventually put on sale.

Two motives inspired this violent diatribe disguised as a preface; one was personal and the other political. From the former point of view, Campoamor ridiculed a philosophical school which, quite aside from any judgment of it and the mere fact that it existed at the time, rendered absurd Campoamor's efforts to be considered a notable philosopher. Not content with the fact that the taste of the period allowed him to pass for a famous bard, worthy of rubbing elbows in Parnassus with Goethe himself, he also wanted to have incense burned to him as a thinker, not only because he had cast into doggerel the philosophical systems of Schelling, Cabanis, Heraclitus, Democritus, and others,[9] but also because he had composed in good Spanish prose treatises like *El personalismo* and *Lo absoluto*.[10] But all in vain. The Krausists simply did not take him seriously. They praised the poet ungrudgingly, for after all they shared the distorted notion of lyric poetry held at the time; but they went no further than that. Giner expressed in a review of *Lo absoluto* what was undoubtedly the general opinion of his colleagues: 'Method, proof, precision, discipline, are alien to the famous poet; and in general his procedure does not depart one jot from that which he employed in his best *Doloras*...And the fact is that – the author himself admits it – "it is much easier to think freely than logically".'[11] Giner's scorn, though sweetened with courtesy, was nevertheless obvious. Campoamor was not to forget it.

The second motive was even less pardonable, for it sprang from the desire to ingratiate himself with the most obtuse and arrogant group in the new political situation. Now it was the Marquis of Orovio, Minister of Public Works, and the stubborn reactionaries he represented, to whom Campoamor addressed a fervent apology. During the first few months of the monarchy Campoamor had felt apprehensive. No one could predict whether the new regime would turn in the direction of moderation and harmony or toward that of the most flagrant reaction, though Orovio's decrees seemed to suggest a possible victory by the intransigent faction. And Campoamor pusillanimously decided to draw all possible official suspicion away from himself. In earlier days he had been a judge at examinations for university chairs and had given his vote to candidates who were Krausists. The possibility that such actions might now be interpreted as proof of complicity in Krausist 'machinations' led him to seek pardon from the reactionaries even at the cost of personal dignity. The moderate response given to his caustic preface by Canalejas merely served to exasperate its author.[12] It is incredible that, only a month after the Krausist professors had been dismissed and exiled, any member of the school was left to defend his persecuted colleagues. The letter published by Campoamor on 23 May 1875 comes close to indecency on the one hand and abjection on the other. To the Krausists he says that they are 'trying to convert science into a barrier against governmental authority'; that 'it is impossible to deal with Krausism without appearing to be writing about politics, and socialist politics at that, for from the redoubt of harmonic rationalism cannons aimed by gunners full of good intentions are ever in readiness against every social order...those good intentions which, it is said, pave the road to hell'; that ethics is impossible within their system; that Sanz del Río suffered from 'intellectual strabismus' and that his disciples 'have set back philosophical education in Spain by at least a hundred years'. And, with his eyes turned toward Orovio, he ends his attack with a paragraph that deserves to be transcribed in full:

I declare that the fire from heaven which they say God loosed on the cities of the plain, would seem to me little enough to wipe out these Babels of human understanding...eternal foci of intellectual and moral intoxication. What! A beggar is not allowed to exchange a counterfeit coin that he has innocently received from another without falling under the rules of the Penal Code; and are we to permit exchange of the coins of obviously false doctrines, which carry confusion to all kinds of ideas, to government, to family, to religion and art; converting government into anarchy; the family into a chance association unconnected with God; religion to a formless pantheism, and art to limitless chaos?[13]

Later, when the controversy had deteriorated into sheer absurdity, Campoamor was to say that 'it is a proof of *very good taste* in the Cánovas ministry to know whether there is an attempt in the Universities to turn into *science* what is *mutiny* on the streets, and whether the *rumor of certain ideas* may easily become a *tumult of events*'.[14] Like Navarro Villoslada and the anti-Krausists of 1865–1867, Campoamor appealed to governmental fiat to do away with the hated doctrine. His attitude was not only intellectually unworthy and morally offensive, it was politically mistaken. What had been possible in the political climate of 1867 was no longer possible in 1875. Despite Orovio's return to the Ministry of Public Works, intellectual repression formed no part of Cánovas's plans, for as a civil politician he was more interested in harmony than antagonism. Campoamor's campaign subsided, in the end, into an undignified and ineffective demand for reprisals.

6. Menéndez Pelayo and Spanish science

In April, 1876, Marcelino Menéndez Pelayo, at the time a stripling of twenty, entered the arena for the first time to wield the weapons of history against Gumersindo de Azcárate, the champion *par excellence* of harmonic rationalism. An occasion for battle was offered by the ex-professor of the University of Madrid with the publication, in *Revista de España*, of a series of essays entitled *El self-government y la monarquía doctrinaria*.[15] One of them, which dealt with matters of constitutional law, contained the following statement: 'According to whether, for example, the State defends or denies freedom of knowledge, so a nation's energy will display more or less of its peculiar genius in this field, and there might even be a case in which its activity would be almost completely stifled, as has happened in Spain for three centuries.'[16] This opinion, considering the moment when it appeared, is certainly not very novel; furthermore, its obvious incidental nature, of something written in the heat of composition, is proof of the statement's general currency. The strangulation of intellectual activity in Spain by absolutism and the Inquisition was an indispensable refrain in every dirge sung about national decadence. This arouses the suspicion that it was not the statement itself, but rather its author's ideological orientation, that moved Gumersindo Laverde, professor of literature at the University of Valladolid, to demand that his fellow-townsman and learned disciple refute it. And indeed, on 30 April 1876 Menéndez Pelayo published in the *Revista Europea* a letter to Laverde which opened the famous controversy on scientific activity in Spain.[17]

However, it happens that the text chosen to impugn the well-worn thesis is ambiguous. For from what point should the three centuries to which Azcárate referred be counted? Would it not be desirable to elucidate this point before rushing into the fray? Menéndez Pelayo had no hesitation in doing so. In the first place, he assumed that the centuries in question were the sixteenth, seventeenth, and eighteenth. He conveniently overlooked the fact that Azcárate had not said 'as happened in Spain', relegating the action to a categorical position in the past, but 'as has happened in Spain', in the belief that this meant that the situation he deplored had continued almost up to the present. Now, that present was the year 1876, which initiated the last quarter of the nineteenth century. Azcárate was more than justified, therefore, when he later insisted that 'when I said "for three centuries" I meant the last years of the sixteenth, the seventeenth and eighteenth, and the early years of the present century, thus leaving out,' he added, 'or such was my desire, the scientific achievements of the sixteenth century'.[18] Was this an insignificant detail? Not at all. Note that, if almost all of the sixteenth century was in fact excluded from this three-century period of time, Menéndez Pelayo had no excuse for attacking Azcárate, especially since, as he himself admitted, in philosophy the seventeenth century – though memorable for other reasons – was a 'degenerate sequel' to the preceding one; and as for the eighteenth century, it need only be said that during it 'all foreign doctrines, good or bad, useful or harmful, penetrated Spain without opposition'. in order to realize, by indirect testimony, how meager and feeble Spanish intellectual efforts were.[19] And so it was indispensable for the attacker to include the sixteenth century in the period of paralysis lamented by Azcárate, even at the risk of interpreting his words incorrectly. Doubtless in honor of the noble cause for which he had taken up his pen, the learned youth did not shrink from (a) stating gratuitously that the Krausists considered Spanish intellectual activity 'null' until Sanz del Río imported harmonic rationalism from Germany; and (b) deliberately seeking a quarrel with a man whose reputation was such as to assure that the debate would be well publicized.[20]

At least in its early stages, the controversy about Spanish science was not provoked 'out of the fullness of the heart', nor did it have the characteristics of a hasty reply to a statement which is felt to be intolerable and demands immediate and vigorous refutation. The 'astonishment' and 'ill-humor' which Menéndez Pelayo says Azcárate's declaration caused him seem as unspontaneous as the comments set down 'at top speed of my pen and almost without consulting books' into which his anger was vented. The attack on Azcárate and, through him, on the Krausists and other so-called 'denigrators' of national science, was premeditated. But the tactic left a good deal to be desired. The dual intention to smash his adversary and to prove that there had been Spanish science during that three-century period made the refutation in large measure ineffective, precisely owing to an excess of proof. Menéndez Pelayo sent forth brigades of names and battalions of titles against his antagonist, as if the success of the attack depended on the numbers of his troops rather than on clear judgment. It must be remembered that the authors and writings adduced in support of his position were chosen 'among a thousand others which', adds the attacker, 'I omit at present'. In view of this, the reader is perplexed: How is it that there were so many cultivators of science in Spain of whose names all trace has been lost? And if they existed and were forgotten, did they not perhaps deserve to be forgotten? And if they did not deserve to be forgotten and were forgotten, is not this oblivion sufficient proof of a gradual blunting of scientific activity? In any case, would it not have been preferable for the attacker to sacrifice this flood of names in favor of a handful of really valuable scientists, and, having done so, to describe the extent of their contributions and the influence of this nucleus of superior minds? This is precisely what a mature and sedate Menéndez Pelayo was to do, with consummate skill, in the course of time; but at the age of twenty fairness is less desirable than devotion to a cause, especially when that devotion is nourished by patriotic fervor.

The reader is left in his perplexity until at last he realizes that Spanish science is not the real subject of controversy. The subject is Spain. At the root of the question, as a source of emotional excitement, lies 'patriotic affection',[21] exacerbated during this time by the bankruptcy of many hopes, by nostalgia for a golden past, by disappointment with the present, by lack of confidence in the future. What made Menéndez Pelayo take up his pen was 'that disdain for everything domestic, those antipatriotic statements which afflict and sadden the soul'. Some years later, in commenting on a speech in which Núñez de Arce attributed the national decline to religious intolerance, the future great scholar was to write, 'I do not envy him the sad glory of upholding such an antipatriotic and backward cause.' The controversy, then, was about Spain, and what that really means is that there was a controversy against one Spain – that of the adversaries – in the name of another which alone was considered genuine – one's own Spain. Each intellectual faction projected on the national map, with pretensions to exclusivity, the particular image of Spain that it was defending. Some turned to a vociferous kind of patriotism to annihilate the adversary, forgetting that along with the sort of patriotism which promotes noble aims, there is another, narrower patriotism which, instead of joining individual wills in a common affirmation, separates them in reciprocal suspicion. Menéndez Pelayo would say, for example, in the name of one Spain, that the *Revista Contemporánea* was not Spanish, though its editor and contributors were Spaniards, 'no doubt', he adds, 'by mistake', and would proclaim that he considered it 'an anti-Catholic, antinational, and antiliterary undertaking'. Revilla would write, in the name of another Spain, that Menéndez Pelayo was 'the implacable enemy of civilization and the motherland'. Such anathemas were numerous, unfortunately, and we need not multiply them here. The Spanish intellectual, victim of the general hyperaesthesia, used his pen like a dart and his words like rockets.

Perhaps for this very reason the attitude of one man who avoided diatribe, even at the risk of seeming spiritless, stands out all the more. And in the controversy over Spanish science the only man who offered an example of moderation was Azcárate. Why did the Krausist writer have no reply to the challenge offered by Menéndez Pelayo? Was it out of disdain for the then-obscure bibliographer from Santander, as Menéndez Pelayo and his teacher Laverde tried to imply? Out of fear of a possible defeat? No, he remained silent simply out of patriotism. In schismatic periods, *nolo contendere* can also be a patriotic attitude. 'I did not speak out', wrote Azcárate to Laverde, 'because I wished and hoped that the controversy would be carried on by persons more expert, and more given to such studies, than I; and especially I did not speak out because the glories of our country were involved, and it repelled me a little to seem to be disputing these.'[22] And the following declaration is one of profound patriotism, of thirst for harmony:

There are so many things which separate men these days, that it is a pleasure to reduce their number and increase the number of things which unite us. This is why, since we have different opinions about our country's scientific life in the seventeenth and eighteenth centuries and the causes of her prostration, it is well to establish the fact that neither party denies the sixteenth century's glorious philosophical tradition, and that all of us desire the formation and development of *Spanish Philosophy*.[23]

With Azcárate out of the fray, Menéndez Pelayo turned on other supporters of 'antipatriotic causes'. In response to either direct or oblique provocations, Revilla, Salmerón, and Perojo entered the lists. Revilla insisted that, no matter what Laverde and his disciple might say, Spanish philosophy was 'a myth'. Salmerón proclaimed that Spain's scientific indigence was attributable to the slight influence that the Renaissance and Reformation had exercised on the Spanish intellect. Perojo tried to demonstrate 'in a conclusive and decisive way... that the Inquisition paralyzed the whole scientific movement of our nation'. The tactic employed by Menéndez Pelayo against these antagonists was the same he had used with Azcárate, with the difference that the general tone was more intemperate, perhaps because the new adversaries were more experienced in the cut-and-thrust of verbal combat. In this second and more virulent phase the controversy lasted well into 1877. In the spring of that year Menéndez Pelayo was in Italy, absorbed, during the hours he succeeded in snatching from his bibliographical labors, in the works of that Renaissance, fusion of the best of classical antiquity and the Christian spirit, which was the great love of his life. But not so absorbed that he forgot his adversaries in Madrid, 'the perpetual enemies of Religion and the motherland'. From Venice on 6 and 8 May 1877, and from Milan on the ninth of that month, he wrote to Alejandro Pidal a long refutation – more than seventy pages – of an essay José del Perojo had published in the *Revista Contemporánea* under the title of *La ciencia española bajo la Inquisición*.[24] With this parting shot the young scholar ended the controversy.

And, after all is said and done, what was established by so many pros and cons about Spanish science? That those who took part in the controversy embodied three different ways of interpreting and evaluating Spain's intellectual history. Even without referring to other clues, each one of those attitudes allows us to identify very accurately the overall ideological configuration of the person associated with it. Menéndez Pelayo, installed in the valley of the present, looks back at the peaks of the past and insists: Spanish intellect was everything it should have been. Azcárate, for his part, entrenched in his ideal, proclaims: Spain's intellectual life was not everything it might have been. And lastly, Revilla and Perojo, imaginary tenants of an imaginary better future, announce: Spanish science was nothing very grand. Traditionalism, rationalism, and progressivism simply repeat at the tops of their voices their respective historical postulates.

As for the subject of the controversy, perhaps it would be best to quote the opinion of another famous polemicist – a polemicist even with himself – Miguel de Unamuno:

I always believed that there has never been true philosophy in Spain; but since I read the works of Señor Menéndez y Pelayo, which aim to prove to us that there had indeed been Spanish philosophy, my last doubts were dissipated and I became completely convinced that until now the Spanish people have been impervious to all truly philosophical comprehension. I became convinced of it when I saw that commentators or expositors of other philosophies, scholars and students of philosophy, are called philosophers. And I was finally confirmed, corroborated, and clinched in my opinion when I saw that the name of philosopher was given to such writers as Balmes, Father Ceferino González, Sanz del Río, and still others... When I have heard someone uphold the historical absurdity that Spanish thought was lost in past centuries because it spent too much time on theology, and add that we have lacked physicists, chemists, mathematicians, or physiologists because we have had a superabundance of theologians, I have always said the same thing, and it is that in Spain, just as there have never been philosophers, and precisely because there never have been, there have been no theologians either, but only expositors, commentators, vulgarizers, and scholars of theology.[25]

Afterword

In trying to judge Spanish Krausism, posterity has swung between two opposite opinions. One reduces it to a philosophical doctrine which, fed by a tortuous metaphysic, attracted a handful of persons interested in the abstruse or the bizarre. Another maintains the view that it is incorrect, strictly speaking, to refer to Krausism as if it were a philosophical 'school', for Krause's doctrine assumed a very personal character in each of its Spanish followers. Equidistant between these points of view is the opinion of those who have viewed Krausism as a system of ethics pure and simple, and its partisans as a group of moralists determined to reform both man and society. Those who hold this opinion allege, as proof of their assertion, that disciplines having to do with human conduct – law, sociology, pedagogy – are precisely those which have obtained the greatest and most lasting benefits from the Spanish Krausists' contributions.

On my part, I have so far avoided expressing a general judgment. In the preceding chapters I have confined myself to examining those aspects I have thought necessary in order to understand what Spanish Krausism tried to be, and in fact was, during the period – approximately 1854–1874 – of its maximum influence. We can hardly deny that the meaning we attribute to some of its aspects may be arguable; but neither can we deny that everything associated with that period in the spiritual history of the past century lends itself to debate. What is not at all arguable is the fact that Spanish Krausism was a good deal more than a metaphysic, or an ethical doctrine, or a complete philosophical system. Had it merely been one of these things, its influence would have been restricted to a small intellectual circle and its significance would be purely historical: a fleeting phase in the chronicle of modern Spanish thought. But no one, not even the most vehement detractor of Krausist doctrine, would dare to state that its influence ceased with the breakup of Sanz del Río's group of disciples during the early days of the

Restoration, or with the later defection of a few of them. And why was this so? Simply because Spanish Krausism was, let us repeat, more than a philosophy; really it was what, for lack of a better expression, we will have to call a 'style of life', a certain way of concerning oneself with life and occupying oneself with it, of thinking it and living it, using reason as a compass to explore, surely and systematically, the whole of creation. There is no doubt that between Sanz del Río and Fernando de Castro, or between Salmerón and Giner, different orientations can be observed. But there is also no doubt that these men, and their companions in intellectual adventure, shared the same confidence in reason as the standard of life and displayed an identical taste for certain subjects in the spiritual repertory of the eighteenth century. All of them believed in man's perfectibility, in the progress of society, in the essential beauty of life. They all worked ardently for a better world. But there is something more. 'Should we wish to characterize all of them by a common trait,' writes Azorín of the Krausists:

we would say that all the men who form part of this group and this period are distinguished by a zeal, a sincere longing, to learn, to know; and to their longing and desire to know and explore the regions of thought, they add a rectitude, a probity, a sincerity, which can be considered as fundamental, as typical, in the historical period during which that intellectual movement unfolded.

Notes

Chapter 1. Julián Sanz del Río

1. 'Discurso pronunciado en la Universidad Central por el doctor D. Julián Sanz del Río, profesor de Historia de la Filosofía en la Facultad de Filosofía y Letras, en la solemne inauguración del año académico de 1857 a 1858', in *Ideal de la Humanidad para la vida*, 2nd ed., Madrid, 1871, pp. 293–347. The text of this address has been reproduced in J. Sanz del Río, *Textos escogidos* (preface by Eloy Terrón), Barcelona, 1968, pp. 171–225.
2. *Ibid.*, pp. 344–345.
3. The adaptation is very free, and the plan followed by Sanz del Río quite different from that of Krause's book. In some sections Sanz del Río's contribution is so considerable that many Krausists thought of the *Ideal* as an original work by the Spanish professor. Giner says that in Sanz del Río's book 'there is hardly more of Krause than the free inspiration of thought'. The edition to which these notes refer is the second edition, Madrid, 1871, printed by order of Sanz del Río's literary executors.
4. *Ibid.*, p. 126.
5. For the resemblances between Hegel and Comte in this respect see John T. Merz, *A History of European Thought in the Nineteenth Century*, Edinburgh–London, 1896–1914, IV, pp. 186–187. Friedrich Jodl says of Krause and Comte, 'not only in [their] belief in moral progress..., but also in many external details, this analogy can be observed: preference for the didactic form of the catechism, for the extremely detailed exposition of principles; the arid and equivocal terminology, loaded with newly-invented technical terms. Both thought of themselves as prophets in this world...' And he adds: 'The ethics of both men tends to proclaim a religion of humanity which appears in the one under metaphysical form, in the other under positivist form; now confining itself to the given world and the knowable connections among things, now extending man's thoughts and actions, in ambitious flight, beyond the frontiers of the universe.' *Geschichte der Ethik*, 2nd ed., II, pp. 102–103.
6. Menéndez Pelayo, M., *Historia de los heterodoxos españoles*, Madrid, 1946–1948, VI, p. 275.
7. In a letter to José de la Revilla, written from Heidelberg in 1844, Sanz del Río says, 'as it was necessary...to become familiar with the German language [in order to study Krause's philosophy], I came to this city...' 'Cartas inéditas de don Julián Sanz del Río', in *Revista Europea*, I, 3 (15 March 1874), p. 66.
8. *Ibid.*, p. 68.
9. See Chapter 6.

10. Doubly unfortunate if it is remembered that the University of Göttingen, founded in 1734 and inaugurated in 1737, was the first to proclaim the principle of *libertas docendi*. See V. Paulsen, *Geschichte des gelehrten Unterrichts auf den deutschen Schulen und Universitäten*, Leipzig, 1885, pp. 424–425.

11. *Compendio de la Historia Universal*, by Dr G. Weber, Madrid, 1853, 2 vols. (Antigüedad y Edad Media); *Compendio doctrinal de la Historia Universal hasta 1852*, Madrid, 1855–1856, 2 vols. (Renacimiento y Revoluciones).

12. Menéndez Pelayo, *Heterodoxos...*, VI, pp. 385–386.

13. 'Sobre el concepto que hoy se forma de España', in *Revista de España*, I, I (1868), pp. 46–70.

14. Sanz del Río, 'Discurso...', p. 313.

Chapter 2. Harmonic rationalism

1. On Krause and harmonic rationalism the following works can be consulted: Paul Hohlfeld, *Die Krause'sche Philosophie*, Dresden, 1879; A. Procksch, *K. Ch. F. Krause: Ein Lebensbild nach seinen Briefen*, Leipzig, 1880; Rudolf Eucken, *Zur Erinnerung an K. Ch. F. Krause*, Leipzig, 1881; Friedrich Jodl, *Geschichte der Ethik in der neueren Philosophie*, Stuttgart, 1882–1889; Clay MacCauley, *K. Ch. F. Krause: Heroic Pioneer for Thought and Life*, Berkeley, 1925; and the general histories of Erdmann, Ueberweg, and Zeller. The book by Krause which includes almost all aspects of the harmonic system, though simplifying them somewhat, is *Vorlesungen über die Grundwahrheiten der Wissenschaft*, Göttingen, 1829; Prague, 1868 (2nd ed.).

2. This summary includes only the easily accessible parts of Krausist philosophy. My interest in it, with regard to its manifestations in Spain, lies chiefly in its role as an intellectual catalyst rather than a system of thought; and hence I stress only that part of the doctrine which, owing to its prescriptive and reformist character, actually influenced Spanish minds in the second half of the nineteenth century. But this is precisely the least formal and technical part of Krause's thought. Even in his most faithful disciples there is an obvious preference for the 'practical' side – understood in its broadest sense – of the harmonic system. Ahrens and Röder are interested almost exclusively in the philosophy of law; Leonhardi in philosophy of history; Tiberghien in philosophy of religion; Hohlfeld in ethics. Only Sanz del Río was interested in Krausist metaphysics, precisely the most perishable part of the system.

3. However, faith does occupy a relevant place in Krausist philosophy. See Hermann von Leonhardi, 'Sätze zu einer vergleichenden Betrachtung des Glaubens und des Wissens, der Wissenschaft und der Religion', in *Die neue Zeit*, II (1870). This essay was translated into Spanish by Francisco Giner de los Ríos and included, under the title of 'Religión y ciencia', in *Estudios filosóficos y religiosos*, Madrid, 1876, pp. 217–297.

4. Krause, *Urbild der Menschheit*, Dresden, 1811, p. 28; Sanz del Río, *Ideal...*, pp. xii, 33–35.

5. Eucken, *op. cit.*, pp. 44–45; *Grundwahrheiten...*, pp. 93 *et seq.*

6. Jodl, *op. cit.*, pp. 91–101.

7. Henri-Frédéric Amiel, *Journal intime*, Geneva, 1923. Entry of 19 June 1872.

8. Eucken, *op. cit.*, pp. 52–53; Krause, *Grundwahrheiten...*, pp. 484 *et seq.*

9. Eucken, *op. cit.*, pp. 19 *et seq.*

10. Krause, *Grundwahrheiten...*, p. 564.

11. Krause, *Urbild*, pp. 28 *et seq.*; Sanz del Río, *Ideal...*, pp. 27 *et seq.* Hence-

forward all references will be to the Spanish adaptation of this book of Krause's written by Sanz del Río.

12. *Ideal...*, pp. 240–255.
13. *Ibid.*, pp. 282–284.
14. *Ibid.*, pp. 243–248.
15. *Ibid.*, p. 248.
16. *Ibid.*, p. 250.
17. *Ibid.*, pp. 250–251.
18. *Ibid.*, p. 277.

Chapter 3. Catechumens and nonconformists

1. 'Revista crítica', in *Revista Contemporánea*, xiv (30 March 1878), p. 247. It is, however, true that at this time Revilla was an enthusiast of neo-Kantianism and lost no opportunity to annoy his former fellow-Krausists. As early as 1875 he had declared that he rejected 'the excesses committed [by the Krausists], as unjustified as they are enormous...against the Spanish language'. For the lexical and syntactical obscurities that plague Sanz del Río's philosophical writings, see his Letter No. iii to José de la Revilla in 'Cartas inéditas...', *Revista Europea*, i, 7 (12 April 1874), pp. 193–194. Also see M. Méndez Bejarano, *Historia de la filosofía en España*, Madrid, n.d., pp. 467–469; V. Barrantes, 'Las deformaciones literarias de la filosofía de Krause', in *Revista Europea*, vii, 110 (2 April 1876), pp. 193–198; M. Menéndez Pelayo, *Heterodoxos...*, vi, pp. 386–389; Miguel de Unamuno, 'Sobre la lengua española', in *Ensayos*, Madrid, 1945, i, pp. 328–329, and 'Contra el purismo', in *ibid.*, pp. 410–411.
2. *Revista Europea*, i, 3 (15 March 1874), p. 65.
3. On Sanz del Río, see: Gervasio Manrique, *Sanz del Río*, Madrid, n.d.; Pierre Jobit, *Les Éducateurs de l'Espagne contemporaine*, Paris-Bordeaux, 1936, 2 vols.; J. B. Trend, *The Origins of Modern Spain*, Cambridge-New York, 1934, pp. 30–49; M. Méndez Bejarano, *op. cit.*, pp. 390 *et seq.*; M. Menéndez Pelayo, *op. cit.*, pp. 366 *et seq.*; Federico Sánchez Escribano, 'Julián Sanz del Río', in *Columbia Dictionary of Modern European Literature*, New York, 1947; José Ferrater Mora, 'Sanz del Río, Julián', in *Diccionario de Filosofía*, Madrid, 1979 (6th ed.), 4 vols.; Julián Marías, 'El pensador de Illescas', in *Obras completas*, Madrid, 1959, iv, pp. 480 *et seq.* There is also a select bibliography in Elías Díaz, *La filosofía social del krausismo*, Madrid, 1973, and in Fernando Martín Buezas, *La teología de Sanz del Río y del krausismo español*, Madrid, 1977. Special mention must be made of Pablo de Azcárate, *Sanz del Río (1814–1869)*, Madrid, 1969, owing to the many documents it offers.
4. Quoted in Manrique, *op. cit.*
5. B. Pérez Galdós, *La familia de León Roch*, in *Obras completas*, Madrid, 1941, iv, p. 898. Also see my essay 'Galdós y el krausismo: *La familia de León Roch*', in *Hacia el 98: Literatura, sociedad, ideología*, Barcelona, 1972, pp. 79–118.
6. Menéndez Pelayo, among others, makes this comment: 'When they [the Krausists] were in the saddle, they distributed university chairs like the spoils of battle.' This is a gratuitous statement, like so many others made by the famous scholar when he attacked the Krausist school. Most of the Krausist professors earned their chairs by competitive examination before the Revolution of September, 1868, when the politicians who favored the Krausist movement came to power. *Heterodoxos...*, p. 386.

7. The relationship between Krause and German freemasonry, which was far from untroubled, has been dealt with in fairly detailed form in MacCauley, *op. cit.*, pp. 9–10 and 19–21.
8. Letter No. I, in *Revista Europea*, I, 3 (15 March 1874), p. 68.
9. *Ibid.*, p. 66.
10. Letter No. VII, in *ibid.*, I, 9 (26 April 1874), p. 260.
11. *Ibid.*, p. 260.
12. On Fernando de Castro, see Chapter 7, sect. 4, and my essay 'Una crisis de la conciencia española: krausismo y religión', in *Hacia el 98...*, pp. 129–137.
13. Letter No. VI, in *ibid.*, p. 259.
14. Letter No. VII, in *ibid.*, p. 260.
15. *Ibid.*, p. 260.

Chapter 4. Toward a better world

1. On this point, see the section entitled 'Von der Erkenntnis Gottes und von dem Einfluss derselben auf Gesinnung und Leben', in *Grundwahrheiten...*, pp. 159 *et seq.*
2. Sanz del Río, *Ideal...*, p. 28.
3. *Ibid.*, pp. xii, 30–31, and 33–35.
4. *Ibid.*, p. 27.
5. *Ibid.*, p. 29.
6. *Ibid.*, p. xii.
7. *Ibid.*, pp. xxi–xxii.
8. *Ibid.*, pp. xiii–xiv.
9. *Ibid.*, p. xv.
10. *Ibid.*, pp. xvi–xvii.
11. Decree by the Congregation of the Index, 26 September 1865.
12. 'Positivism is coming into Spain through two doors, one opened by those who work in the natural sciences and the other by the neo-Kantians. Perhaps the efforts of the former group are more effective than those of the people who, in earlier times, worked in medical sciences and tried to spread a similar doctrine.' Gumersindo de Azcárate, 'El positivismo y la civilización', in *Revista Contemporánea*, IV (30 June 1876), note p. 234. Azcárate is referring to the famous Doctors Cortezo and Simarro.
13. See Chapter 5, sect. 4.
14. See my article 'Unamuno and Pascal: Notes on the Concept of Agony', in *Publications of the Modern Language Association of America*, LVI, 6 (1950), pp. 1005–1006. The Spanish version of this study was published in my book *Intelectuales y espirituales*, Madrid, 1961, pp. 41–69.
15. Sanz del Río, *Ideal...*, p. 18.
16. *Ibid.*, p. 15.
17. Nicolás Salmerón, 'La libertad de enseñanza', in *Boletín-Revista de la Universidad de Madrid*, I, 1 (10 January 1869), p. 10.
18. Sanz del Río, *Ideal...*, p. 15.
19. *Ibid.*, pp. 15–16.
20. *Ibid.*, p. 33.
21. *Ibid.*, p. 35.
22. Francisco Giner de los Ríos, *La persona social*, Madrid, 1899, p. 40.
23. Sanz del Río, *Ideal...*, pp. 99–102. Sanz del Río's *Commandments* were based on the precepts for humanization of the individual given by Krause in

Tageblatt des Menschheitlebens, Dresden, 1811. These precepts were published later in his book *Vorlesungen über das System der Philosophie*, Göttingen, 1828 (2nd ed. Prague, 1868). Guillaume Tiberghien, another of Krause's disciples, paraphrased them in *Les Commandements de l'Humanité, ou la vie morale sous forme de catéchisme populaire, d'après Krause*, Brussels, 1872, a work translated into Spanish by A. García Moreno, *Los Mandamientos de la Humanidad*, Madrid, 1874.

24. Menéndez Pelayo, in *Heterodoxos...*, VI, p. 390, calls them 'a ridiculous parody of God's Law'.

Chapter 5. Germanophilia

1. As part of his lengthy *Geschichte der Poesie und Beredsamkeit*, Göttingen, 1801–1819. The section dealing with Spain was translated into Spanish, with additions, by José Gómez de la Cortina and Nicolás Hugalde y Molinedo: *Historia de la literatura española*, Madrid, 1829.
2. *Spanischen Dramen*, 4 vols., Berlin, 1841–1844.
3. *Volkslieder und Romanzen der Spanier im Versmasse des Originals verdeutscht*, Berlin, 1843.
4. *Geschichte der dramatischen Literatur und Kunst in Spanien*, 3 vols., Berlin, 1845–1846.
5. Admiration for Germany, especially in the twenty-year period that preceded the Franco-Prussian War, is shown in expressions such as 'cultured Germany', 'learned Germany', 'erudite Germany', so frequently encountered in books and periodicals of the time.
6. 'El Panenteísmo', in *Revista Europea*, IV, 67 (6 June 1875), p. 531.
7. 'our Lemming [dictionary] was assaulted by those of us who wanted to learn the language of Schiller and Goethe. As Sanz del Río said, most of us turned back at the threshold...', *Ibid.*, p. 531.
8. The Spanish version of both works was owed to A. García Moreno, a translator as prolific as he was careless. He also translated into Spanish, always by way of French texts, works by Max Müller, Draper, Bluntschli, etc.
9. Rafael Montoro complains that in Spain periodical publications have not followed closely the development of German science and philosophy, a situation very different from that which obtains 'in France and England [where] books and magazine articles, all worthy of special mention, have...followed German thought in its movement through all spheres of intellectual activity'. 'El movimiento intelectual en Alemania', in *Revista Europea*, V, 86 (17 October 1875), p. 631.
10. *Análisis del pensamiento racional*, Madrid, 1877, note p. xv.
11. V. Barrantes, 'Las deformaciones literarias de la filosofía de Krause', in *Revista Europea*, VII, 110 (2 April 1876), p. 197.
12. 'Discurso...' in *Ideal...*, pp. 337, 339.
13. *Ibid.*, p. 340.
14. Included in F. Giner, *Estudios filosóficos y religiosos*, Madrid, 1876, pp. 1–24. The essay was written in 1871.
15. *Ibid.*, p. 2.
16. *Ibid.*, pp. 6–7. Sanz del Río furnishes us with an excellent distinction between *Wissenschaft* and *science* in the French-Spanish sense of the word: 'Do not confuse empirical knowledge, and much less the science of the world called positive, with Knowledge and Systematic Science. The first of these is an incomplete science, the second a full and healthy exercise of the Spirit; the

Science of laws is light, that of facts is movement; the former is the root, the latter the fruit. Facts bring themselves to our observation; we must build Science within ourselves...; Science builds conviction according to permanent laws which govern all the facts of a single kind.' 'Discurso...', pp. 334–335.

17. See Chapter 2, sect. 2.

18. *Estudios filosóficos...*, p. 10.

19. *Ibid.*, p. 13.

20. Between 1871 and 1875 Giner gave a series of free lectures on the Theory of Science at the University of Madrid, perhaps the best presentation in Spain of the organic concept of *Wissenschaft*. The series was interrupted by Orovio's decrees and Giner's subsequent banishment to Cádiz. The scope of the lectures can be studied in 'Apuntes para un programa de elementos de doctrina de la ciencia', in his *Estudios filosóficos...*, pp. 85–139. See also, in the same work, 'Fragmento sobre clasificación de las ciencias', pp. 57–83.

21. See J. T. Merz, *History*, I, pp. 35–41.

22. *Ibid.*, I, pp. 159–161.

23. Quoted in *ibid.*, I, p. 160.

24. 'Cartas inéditas', in *Revista Europea*, I, 3 (15 March 1874), p. 69.

25. Fernando de los Ríos, *El pensamiento vivo de Giner*: 'La Universidad española', Buenos Aires, 1949, pp. 156–157. For a more detailed study of Giner's ideas on matters pertaining to the university, see *La universidad española*, in *Obras completas*, II, Madrid, 1916.

26. *Minuta de un testamento*, Madrid, 1876, p. 93.

27. 'La libertad de enseñanza', in *Boletín-Revista de la Universidad de Madrid*, I, 2 (25 January 1869), pp. 57 *et seq.*

28. The chief decrees on educational matters issued by the September Revolution were collected in the *Boletín-Revista de la Universidad de Madrid* and published as an appendix to Vol. II, 1870, under the title *Colección legislativa de Instrucción Pública.*

29. Both began as positivists and later embraced Spencerian evolutionism. Simarro founded an 'Association for the progress of the sciences' and held the chair of experimental psychology at the University of Madrid. He has the honor of being the chief exponent of experimental psychology in Spain. See M. Méndez Bejarano, *op. cit.*, pp. 494–495.

30. *Revista Europea*, II, 56 (21 March 1875), pp. 85–89.

31. *Ibid.*, p. 86.

32. Urbano González Serrano, *Ensayos de crítica y de filosofía*, Madrid, 1881, p. 182. González Serrano must also be included among the intellectual Germanophiles. In the essay referred to above he speaks admiringly of 'a people as cultured as the Germans, where thinkers, scientists, and poets appear with such astonishing ease that one would think Germany has seized the intellectual scepter once and for all, among all nations' (p. 180).

33. *Ensayos sobre el movimiento intelectual en Alemania* (first series), Madrid, 1875.

34. 'Objeto de la filosofía en nuestros tiempos', in *Revista Europea*, II, 70 (27 June 1875), p. 648.

35. And certainly not in the sense of *Wissenschaft*. Compare with the idea expressed by Sanz del Río (see note 16) the following opinion of Perojo's: 'We give the same meaning to the terms "science" and "scientific knowledge", hence believing, as the basis for the existence of everything that might be called scientific, in the reality of any object whatsoever insofar as it is known

to us, and therefore making the truth of what we call science depend on the reality of the object it must study, and on the nature of knowledge'. In 1874 the University of Heidelberg did not give the same meaning to the word *science* as it did in 1844.

36. 'Objeto de la filosofía...', p. 650.

Chapter 6. Gallophobia

1. See Chapter 5, sect. 1.
2. Juan Valera, 'La decadencia de la cultura española después de 1860', an address in response to Gaspar Núñez de Arce's acceptance speech on his reception into the Royal Spanish Academy (21 May 1876). During that same spring of 1876 there had been a debate in the Section of Literature and Fine Arts of the Madrid Athenaeum on the subject of dramatic literature in Spain, and a number of participants in the debate attributed the contemporary decline of the genre to the imitation of French models. Manuel de la Revilla was the person who denounced most violently the 'Frenchified' ways of the period's playwrights. At least Revilla had retained, from his Krausist years, his aversion to French thought and letters. Even his recent conversion to positivism did not cause him to admire August Comte.
3. Letter I, in *Revista Europea*, I, 3 (15 March 1874), p. 68.
4. See Amiel, *op. cit.*, entries of 23 April 1862, 23 May 1873, and 22 January 1875; Benjamin Constant, *Journal intime* [Jean Mistler, ed.], Monaco, 1945, p. 228.
5. 'Cosmópolis lúbrica', in *De esto y de aquello*, Buenos Aires, 1953, III, p. 239. The essay's date is December, 1912.
6. Cf. Amiel: 'So far from being philosophical, the French brain is the exact opposite of a philosophical brain, for it does not permit solving any problem and is incapable of understanding anything that is alive, complex, and concrete. Abstraction is its original sin, presumption its incurable defect, and plausibility its fatal limit.' *Op. cit.*, entry of 22 January 1875.
7. Letter I, p. 68.
8. Included in F. Giner, *Estudios de literatura y arte*, Madrid, 1876, pp. 165–245.
9. See Chapter 2, sect. 5.
10. *Estudios de literatura...*, pp. 166–167.
11. On this point, consult also Giner's essay entitled 'Poesía erudita y poesía vulgar', in *Estudios de literatura...*, pp. 93–103.
12. 'Consideraciones...', p. 177.
13. *Ibid.*, p. 179.
14. *Ibid.*, pp. 177–178.
15. *Ibid.*, p. 178.
16. Giner himself wrote a special historico-critical essay on this subject entitled 'Dos reacciones literarias: Clásicos y románticos', also included in *Estudios de literatura...*, pp. 105–129.
17. 'Consideraciones...', pp. 180–185.
18. *Ibid.*, p. 191.
19. *Ibid.*, pp. 213, 219.

Chapter 7. Krausism and literature

1. Sanz del Río, *Ideal...*, pp. 65, 175; Francisco Giner, 'El arte y las artes', in *Estudios de literatura...*, p. 3.

2. K[rause], 'Estética', in *Boletín-Revista de la Universidad de Madrid*, II, 19 (10 July 1870), pp. 1288 *et seq.*; Hermenegildo Giner, *Teoría de la literatura y de las artes*, Barcelona, n.d., pp. 7 *et seq.*; Sanz del Río, *Ideal*..., pp. 53–55; Francisco Giner, 'Del género de poesía más propio de nuestro siglo', in *Estudios de literatura*..., pp. 48–49. See also the prologue to my book *Krausismo: Estética y literatura*, Barcelona, 1973.
3. F. Giner, 'Del género...', p. 49.
4. *Ibid.*, p. 49.
5. Sanz del Río, *Ideal*..., p. 64: 'Artistic life is in every way human, original life, nourished by the spirit's internal conceptions.'
6. 'Del género...', p. 47.
7. *Ibid.*, p. 51.
8. 'Consideraciones...', in *Estudios de literatura*..., p. 166.
9. *Ibid.*, p. 168.
10. K[rause], *op. cit.*, pp. 1348 *et seq.*; F. Giner, 'Del género...', pp. 48–49. Considered from a different viewpoint, 'works of art, like Prometheus, bring to earth a ray of infinite beauty; they are a living and gradual revelation of divinity among men'. Sanz del Río, *Ideal*..., p. 55.
11. 'Consideraciones...', p. 169.
12. *Ibid.*, p. 169.
13. *Ibid.*, p. 170.
14. F. Giner, 'Dos reacciones literarias', in *Estudios de literatura*..., pp. 115–116.
15. *Ibid.*, p. 119.
16. 'Del género...', pp. 50–51.
17. F. Giner, *Estudios de literatura*..., p. xii.
18. 'Del género...', pp. 58–59.
19. *Ibid.*, p. 57.
20. H. Giner, *Teoría*..., pp. 81–82. See the prologue to my *Krausismo: Estética*..., pp. 20–25.
21. 'Del género...', p. 60.
22. *Ibid.*, pp. 60–61.
23. '*Galdós*', in *Páginas escogidas*, Madrid, 1917, p. 57.
24. *Ibid.*, p. 58. See my essay 'La Revolución de Septiembre y la novela española', in *Hacia el 98*..., pp. 9–41.
25. 'Doña Perfecta', in González Serrano, *Ensayos de crítica*..., p. 201.
26. See my *Krausismo: Estética*..., pp. 25–30.
27. 'Dos reacciones...', p. 127.
28. 'Consideraciones...', pp. 240–241.
29. *Ibid.*, pp. 241–242.
30. 'Dos reacciones...', p. 127.

Chapter 8. Krausism and religion

1. As early as 1849 Gioacchino Cardinal Pecci, archbishop of Perugia (later Pope Leo XIII), had proposed to the provincial council of Spoleto the adoption of a catalogue of errors condemned by the Church. In 1907 Pius X promulgated a second Syllabus condemning modernism.
2. The *Syllabus* can be divided into nine parts: 1. Pantheism, naturalism, and absolute rationalism (props. 1–7); 2. Moderate rationalism (8–14); 3. Indifferentism and latitudinarianism (15–18); 4. The Church, its rights and privileges (19–38); 5. Secular society in itself and its relations with the

Church (39–55); 6. Natural ethics and Christian ethics (56–64); 7. Marriage (65–74); 8. Temporal sovereignty of the Roman Pontiff (75–76); 9. Modern liberalism (77–80).

3. The latter opinion was that of the group headed by Döllinger. See the series of articles published by the latter in the *Augsburgische Allgemeine Zeitung* from 10 to 15 March 1869. The articles were collected in the book *Der Papst und das Concil*, Leipzig, 1869, published under the pseudonym *Janus* by Döllinger, Huber, and Friedrich.

4. See Menéndez Pelayo, *Heterodoxos...*, VI, pp. 289 *et seq.*

5. See Gustave de Molinari, 'Les Congrès catholiques', in *Revue des Deux Mondes*, 3rd period, XI, 45 (15 September 1875), pp. 411 *et seq.* The portions of Montalembert's speech cited below are taken from this article.

6. These words have often, and erroneously, been attributed to Lacordaire, for example in L. Chaine, *Menus propos d'un catholique libéral*, Paris, n.d., p. 70, and J. C. Bracq, *France Under the Republic*, New York, 1916, p. 308.

7. 'El problema religioso', in *Revista Europea*, IV, 65 (23 May 1875), p. 466.

8. Mendénez Pelayo, *Heterodoxos...*, p. 454.

9. Mendez Bejarano, *Historia de la filosofía...*, p. 481.

10. 'Terrible is blind faith, what we call "the faith of the charcoal-burner". But what is this blind faith after all?'
'What do you believe?'
'What our Holy Mother Church believes and teaches.'
'And what does our Holy Mother Church believe and teach?'
'What I believe (bis).' 'La fe', in *Ensayos*, Madrid, 1945, I, p. 264.

11. 'La ideocracia', in *Ensayos*, I, p. 256.

12. On Fernando de Castro see J. B. Trend, *The Origins of Modern Spain*, Cambridge-New York, 1934, pp. 43 *et seq.*; M. Menéndez Pelayo, *op. cit.*, VI, pp. 396–401 and 468–469; P. Jobit, *op. cit.*, I, pp. 56–57 and 214 *et seq.*; M. Méndez Bejarano, *op. cit.*, p. 472; F. Giner, 'La Iglesia española', in *Estudios filosóficos y religiosos*, Madrid, 1876, pp. 299–341; Azorín, 'Don Fernando de Castro', in *Clásicos y modernos, Obras completas*, Madrid, 1947–1948, II, pp. 810–814; F. Díaz de Cerio, *Fernando de Castro, filósofo de la historia*, León, 1970; José Luis Abellán, 'Estudio preliminar' to Fernando de Castro's *Memoria testamentaria*, Madrid, 1975, with a useful bibliography.

13. Gumersindo de Azcárate, *Minuta...*, p. 37. The portion quoted does not refer directly to Castro, but is applicable to everyone who, like him, abandoned Catholicism after 1870, without, however, renouncing the Christian ideal.

14. F. Giner, *Estudios filosóficos...*, pp. 302–303.

15. *Discurso sobre los caracteres históricos de la Iglesia española*, Madrid, 1866.

16. The condemned proposition reads as follows: 'Romanus Pontifex potest ac debet cum progressu, cum liberalismo et cum recenti civilisatione sese reconciliare et componere.'

17. *Estudios filosóficos...*, p. 305.

18. F. Giner, 'La política antigua y la política nueva', in *Estudios jurídicos y políticos*, Madrid, 1875, p. 151.

19. *Ibid.*, pp. 151–153.

20. Francisco de P. Canalejas, 'La historia de las religiones', in *Revista Europea*, I, 10 (3 May 1874), p. 295.

21. F. Giner, 'Los católicos viejos y el espíritu contemporáneo', in *Estudios filosóficos...*, pp. 345–346.

22. F. Giner, 'La Iglesia española', in *ibid.*, p. 329.
23. Azcárate, *op. cit.*, p. 32, note. All the Krausists are in agreement on this point, following the opinion of Krause.
24. *Ibid.*, p. 31.
25. F. Giner, 'Los católicos viejos...', p. 349.
26. A. Palacio Valdés, *op. cit.*, p. 471. See Canalejas's comments on Schleiermacher in *Las doctrinas religiosas del racionalismo contemporáneo*, Madrid, 1875.
27. This name is given to Catholics who rejected the dogma of papal infallibility decreed by the first Vatican Council. The movement's leaders were Döllinger and Friedrich, both of whom were excommunicated in 1871. After 1872 the dissidents began to form an ecclesiastical organization following the episcopal pattern. See J. F. von Schulte, *Der Altkatholicismus*, Giessen, 1887.
28. 'Los católicos viejos...', p. 348.
29. *Minuta*...See Chapter 9, sect 2.
30. *Ibid.*, pp. 32–33, note.
31. *Ibid.*, p. 64. Canalejas, F. Giner, and later Unamuno also show that they have been influenced by Channing. See my essay 'Una afinidad electiva: G. de Azcárate y W. E. Channing', in *Hacia el 98*...

Chapter 9. Krausism and politics

1. J. Ortega y Gasset, 'Vieja y nueva política', in *Obras completas*, Madrid, 1946– , I, pp. 265–300.
2. *Ibid.*, p. 281.
3. *Clásicos y modernos*, in *Obras completas*, II, p. 898.
4. *Vida y obra de Angel Ganivet*, Madrid, 1925, pp. 59–60.
5. 'Vieja y nueva política', pp. 282–283.
6. Madrid, 1947. Marañón included this preface in his *Ensayos liberales*, Buenos Aires, 1946.
7. *Ibid.*, pp. 13–14.
8. *Ibid.*, p. 15.
9. Madrid, 1948. Also included in *Ensayos liberales*.
10. *Ibid.*, p. 5. Later an opinion very similar to Marañón's is expressed by Juan Marichal, who stresses the 'will for dialogue' as one characteristic of the men of the Restoration. *La españolización de España: La Edad de Oro liberal*, México, 1952, pp. 8–10.
11. *Pensando en España*, in *Obras completas*, V, p. 969.
12. *Madrid*, in *ibid.*, IV, p. 278.
13. *Minuta de un testamento, publicada y anotada por W*..., Madrid, 1876. There is a new edition with an excellent preliminary study by Elías Díaz, Barcelona, 1967. On the *Minuta*, see also the essays 'Galdós y el krausismo: *La familia de León Roch*'; 'Una crisis de la conciencia española: krausismo y religión'; and 'Una afinidad electiva: G. de Azcárate y W. E. Channing' in my *Hacia el 98*..., mentioned above.
14. *Revista Europea*, VI, 139 (22 November 1876), pp. 532–538; VI, 140 (29 November 1876), pp. 563–572.
15. *Ibid.*, p. 532.
16. But lacking the notes. These were added at the last moment so that the manuscript would have enough pages to qualify as a book and hence escape government censorship. Pamphlets, like periodical publications, were at that time subject to press censorship. See Trend, *op. cit.*, p. 178.

17. *Heterodoxos...*, VI, p. 472.
18. *Ibid.*, VI, p. 279.
19. *Minuta...*, p. ix.
20. *Ibid.*, p. 4.
21. 'Don Gumersindo de Azcárate ha muerto', in *Obras completas*, III, p. 11. In the same essay Ortega says of the men of Azcárate's generation: 'they were like survivors of a period that seemed to us more heroic, more energetic, of greater spiritual ferment, which had later suffered a flood of corruption, cynicism, and despair'. On Azcárate, see also Pablo de Azcárate, *Gumersindo de Azcárate: Estudio biográfico documental*, Madrid, 1969, as well as the bibliography presented by Elías Díaz in his book *La filosofía social...*, mentioned above.
22. *Minuta...*, pp. 72–73.
23. *Ibid.*, p. 73.
24. *Ibid.*, p. 75.
25. *Ibid.*, pp. 77–79, note.
26. *Ibid.*, p. 83.
27. *Ibid.*, pp. 83–84.
28. *Ibid.*, p. 85, note.
29. *Ibid.*, p. 87.
30. *Ibid.*, pp. 85–86.
31. Cf. MacCauley, *op. cit.*, pp. 12–15.
32. Azcárate, *El self-government y la monarquía doctrinaria*, Madrid, 1877, pp. 98–101.
33. *Ibid.*, pp. 104–105.

Chapter 10. Spirit of controversy

1. Giner attributes the introduction of neo-Catholicism in Spain to Donoso Cortés. See 'La política antigua y la política nueva', in *Estudios jurídicos...*, p. 72.
2. 'Catholicism's modern champions do not prepare for battle, as its old champions did, by asking heaven for strength amid fervent prayers and harsh penitence; instead they sharpen their tongues on seminary quarrels and make their pens agile with the turbulence of yellow journalism. The apostles and *illuminati* of former days are now irascible polemicists spoiling for a fight; those who formerly enriched the field of religion with their precious blood now drench the arena of debate with bile.' Armando Palacio Valdés, 'Los oradores del Ateneo: Don Miguel Sánchez', in *Revista Europea*, IX, 157 (25 February 1877), p. 248. Cf. Jobit, *op. cit.*, I, pp. 48–49.
3. Jobit, *op. cit.*, I, pp. 48 *et seq.*
4. 'Such is the heap of periodicals of every stamp and size, stuffed with verse and prose, that they are produced even in obscure little towns in the provinces; in living memory there has never been a literary movement in our country similar to that reflected in these periodicals.' Juan Pérez de Guzmán, later to be permanent secretary of the Academy of History, wrote in these terms to Dr H. W. Kronhamm, of Rostock, in 1875. In this letter on 'The literary restoration in Spain', he includes a list of the chief contemporary periodicals published in the provinces. See *Revista Europea*, V, 298 (22 August 1875), p. 302.
5. But only until 1879, the year when José de Cárdenas bought *Revista Contemporánea* and appointed Francisco de Asís Pacheco its editor. After that the

review represented exactly the opposite of what José del Perojo had intended when he founded it. See Ramón Paz, *Revista Contemporánea* (*Madrid, 1875–1907*), Madrid, 1950, whose preface contains much information about the review's history.

6. 'Revista crítica', in *Revista Contemporánea*, I (15 December 1875), pp. 121–128.
7. 'Carta al señor don Ramón de Campoamor', in *Revista Europea*, IV, 67 (6 June 1875), p. 534.
8. *Revista Europea*, IV, 62 (2 May 1875), pp. 321–326.
9. 'with the intention of expanding the limits of poetry's empire... I am putting into verse the philosophical systems of Schelling (*All is one and the same*), Cabanis (*The Café*), Heraclitus, Democritus, Socrates, and Diogenes (*The Comedy of Knowledge*), etc., etc., etc.; but, as it happens, I have never been able to make a single poem out of Krause's system...', said Campoamor in 'Polémica sobre el panenteísmo: ¡A la lenteja, a la lenteja!', in *Revista Europea*, IV, 65 (23 May 1875), p. 441.
10. Published respectively in 1855 and 1865. To these should be added a third book *El Ideísmo*, dated 1883.
11. 'Una dolora en prosa', in *Estudios de literatura...*, pp. 252–253.
12. 'El panenteísmo', in *Revista Europea*, IV, 63 (9 May 1875), pp. 361–364; IV, 67 (6 June 1875), pp. 526–532.
13. *Revista Europea*, IV, 65 (23 May 1875), pp. 441–444.
14. *Revista Europea*, V, 73 (18 July 1875), p. 89.
15. Subsequently published as a book, *El self-government...*, mentioned above.
16. *Ibid.*, p. 114.
17. In its early stage, against Azcárate, Revilla, and Salmerón, this polemic lasted until September, 1876. In its second stage, against Perojo, it was briefly revived in May, 1877. To understand properly the atmosphere in which the polemic occurred, consult the *Epistolario de Laverde Ruiz y Menéndez Pelayo* (edition, notes, and study by Ignacio Aguilera; preface by Sergio Fernández Larrain), Santander, 1967, 2 vols.
18. 'Una carta sobre la filosofía española' [to Gumersindo Laverde], in *Revista Europea*, VIII, 141 (5 November 1876), p. 593.
19. *La ciencia española*, 2nd ed., Madrid, 1879, p. 12.
20. 'Some time ago Señor Menéndez Pelayo amused himself from his provincial home by writing letters to Señor Laverde, in which he deliberately sought the chance to get into a controversy with persons, some of them very well known and others less so, in the world of letters, attacking them in a way that was more than a little uncalled for in one who expected to gain recognition through any of these persons.' José del Perojo, 'La ciencia española bajo la Inquisición', in *Revista Contemporánea*, VIII (15 April 1877), p. 325. Perojo seems to have been right. Menéndez Pelayo begins his article 'Mr. Masson redimuerto' by writing, 'Mr. Masson [Revilla] took the bait, now we have drawn him into the fray.' The provocation is obvious.
21. 'I, who will never avenge slights to myself, have little tolerance for insults to common sense and to our country', *La ciencia...*, p. 139, note.
22. 'Una carta...', p. 592.
23. *Ibid.*, p. 593.
24. 'La ciencia española...', pp. 325–364.
25. 'Sobre la lectura e interpretación del "Quijote"', in *Ensayos*, I, p. 647.

Additional bibliography

Alonso Martínez, M. 'Movimiento de las ideas religiosas en Europa. Exposición y crítica del sistema krausista', *Memorias de la Real Academia de Ciencias Morales y Políticas*, IV (1883), 19–73.

Altamira y Crevea, R. *Biografía intelectual y moral de don Francisco Giner de los Ríos* (Mexico,1955).

Araquistáin, L. 'El krausismo en España', *Cuadernos del Congreso para la Libertad de la Cultura*, XLIV (1960), 5–12.

El pensamiento español contemporáneo (Buenos Aires, 1962).

Azcárate, G. de. *Estudios económicos y sociales* (Madrid, 1876).

Estudios filosóficos y políticos (Madrid, 1877).

El régimen parlamentario en la práctica (Madrid, 1885).

Azorín (J. Martínez Ruiz). 'Lecturas españolas', in *Obras completas*, vol. II (Madrid, 1947).

Cacho Viu, V. *La Institución Libre de Enseñanza. I. Orígenes y etapa universitaria (1860–1881)* (Madrid, 1962).

Calvo Buezas, J. L. *La ética del krausismo español* (Salamanca, 1975).

Canalejas, F. de P. *Estudios críticos de filosofía, política y literatura* (Madrid, 1872).

Doctrinas religiosas del racionalismo contemporáneo. Estudios críticos (Madrid, 1875).

Castro, A. *Semblanzas y estudios españoles* (Madrid, 1956).

Castro, F. de. *Compendio razonado de historia general* (Madrid, 1863–1875), 4 vols.

'Discurso leído en la solemne apertura del curso académico 1868–1869', *Boletín-Revista de la Universidad de Madrid*, I (1869), 22–48.

Cossío, M. B. *De su jornada* (Madrid, 1929).

El Instituto-Escuela de segunda enseñanza (Madrid, 1926).

García Martí V. *El Ateneo de Madrid (1835–1935)* (Madrid, 1948).

Gil Cremades, J. L. *El reformismo español. Krausismo. Escuela histórica. Neotomismo* (Barcelona, 1969).

Krausistas y liberales (Madrid, 1975).

Giner de los Ríos, F. *Obras completas* (Madrid, 1916–1965), 21 vols.

Gómez Molleda, M. D. *Los reformadores de la España contemporánea* (Madrid, 1966).

Jiménez Landi, A. 'Don Francisco Giner de los Ríos y la Institución Libre de Enseñanza', *Revista Hispánica Moderna*, XXV (1959), 1–2, 77p.

La Institución Libre de Enseñanza y su ambiente. Los orígenes (Madrid, 1973).

Labra, R. M. de. *Don Fernando de Castro. Estudio biográfico* (Madrid, 1887).

Luzuriaga, L. *La Institución Libre de Enseñanza y la educación en España* (Buenos Aires, 1957).

Martín Buezas, F. *La teología de Sanz del Río y del Krausismo español* (Madrid, 1977).
Navarro, M. *Vida y obras de don Francisco Giner de los Ríos* (Mexico, 1945).
Orti y Lara, J. M. *Krause y sus discípulos convictos de panteísmo* (Madrid, 1864).
Revilla, J. de la. *Comentarios y notas a las captas inéditas de Sanz del Río* (Madrid, 1854).
Ruiz de Quevedo, M. *La cuestión universitaria* (Madrid, 1876).
Ruiz Salvador, A. *El Ateneo artístico, científico y literario de Madrid (1832–1885)* (London, 1971).
Salmerón y Alonso, N. Preface to G. Tiberghien, *Estudios sobre religión* (Madrid, 1873).
Sanz del Río, J. *Sistema de la Filosofía. Metafísica. Primera parte: Analítica* (Madrid, 1860).
   Sistema de la Filosofía. Metafísica. Segunda parte: Sintética (Madrid, 1874), 2 vols.
   La cuestión de la filosofía novísima (Madrid, 1856).
   Lecciones sobre el sistema de la filosofía analítica de Krause (Madrid, 1868).
Terrón Abad, E. *Sociedad e ideología en los orígenes de la España contemporánea* (Barcelona, 1969).
Tuñón de Lara, M. *Medio siglo de cultura española (1885–1936)* (Madrid, 1970).
   La España del siglo XIX (1808–1914) (Paris, 1968).
Turin, Y. *La educación y la escuela en España de 1874 a 1902. Liberalismo y tradición* (Madrid, 1967).
Xirau, J. *La Institución Libre de Enseñanza. Francisco Giner* (Mexico, 1945).

Index of Names

Ahrens, Heinrich, 5, 7, 30, 51
Alarcón, Pedro Antonio de, 83, 124
Alas, Leopoldo, *see* Clarín
Albareda, José Luis, 57
Alfonso XII, xii, 106, 111
Alonso Martínez, Manuel, 27, 117
Amadeo of Savoy, xii, 111, 113, 118
Amiel, Henri-Frédéric, 1, 7, 16, 66, 67, 141n.
Angoulême, Duke of, 63
Antonelli, Cardinal, 86
Aristotle, 109
Azcárate, Gumersindo de, 56, 98, 99, 100, 103, 105, 106–13, 116, 117, 127, 128–32, 138n.
Azcárate, Patricio de, 108–9
Azorín, 6, 102, 104, 134

Baader, Franz Xaver von, 99
Balmes, Jaime Luciano, 41, 132
Balzac, Honoré de, 82
Barante, Baron de, 50
Barchou de Penhoën, A. T. H., 51
Baroja, Pío, 102
Bartholmès, C. J. G., 51
Baumgarten, Alexander, 85
Bécquer, Gustavo Adolfo, 73
Beethoven, Ludwig van, 69
Bergson, Henri, xvii
Bismarck, Otto von, 93
Böhl de Faber, Juan Nicolás, 49
Bonald, Louis Gabriel de, 114
Bonaparte, Napoleon, 50, 63
Bouterwek, Friedrich, 50
Bretón de los Herreros, Manuel, 73
Bunsen, Christian Karl von, 99

Cabanis, Pierre Jean, 126
Cadalso, José de, 64

Cajal, *see* Ramón y Cajal, Santiago
Calderón, Laureano, 106
Calderón de la Barca, Pedro, 50
Caminero, Francisco Javier, 115
Campoamor, Ramón de, 73, 74, 104, 116, 122, 124–7
Canalejas, Francisco de Paula, 27, 32, 33, 34, 42, 51, 84, 98, 99, 115, 116, 117, 119, 126
Cánovas del Castillo, Antonio, 101, 102, 103, 106, 111, 115, 120, 122, 123, 124, 127
Carlyle, Thomas, 49
Castaños, Francisco Javier, 50
Castelar, Emilio, 102, 115, 120
Castro, Federico de, 84
Castro, Fernando de, xii, xvii, 33, 56, 94–7, 98, 99, 115, 134
Cervantes, Miguel de, 69
Channing, William Ellery, 100
Charles III, x
Charles Albert of Savoy, 91
Clarín, xviii, 82, 103
Coleridge, Samuel Taylor, 49
Comte, Auguste, 59
Conrad, Johannes, 55
Constant, Benjamin, 50, 66
Cortezo, Carlos, 59, 123
Costa, Joaquín, 102, 103, 105, 119
Cousin, Victor, 5, 6, 65, 67

Darwin, Charles, 58
Democritus, 126
Descartes, René, 9, 42
Dickens, Charles, 82
Diez, Friedrich, 50
Döllinger, Johann Joseph, 93, 95
Don Carlos, pretender, x, xi, 113, 114
Dorhn, C. A., 50

For EU product safety concerns, contact us at Calle de José Abascal, 56–1°,
28003 Madrid, Spain or eugpsr@cambridge.org.

www.ingramcontent.com/pod-product-compliance
Ingram Content Group UK Ltd.
Pitfield, Milton Keynes, MK11 3LW, UK
UKHW010048140625
459647UK00012BB/1681